1: PERSPECTIVES IN CRITICISM

PERSPECTIVES IN CRITICISM

1: *Elements of Critical Theory*

1:

Wayne Shumaker

Elements
of Critical Theory

UNIVERSITY OF CALIFORNIA PRESS

Berkeley and Los Angeles

1952

University of California Press
Berkeley and Los Angeles, California
Cambridge University Press
London, England

by the University of California Printing Department
Designed by Ward Ritchie

UXORI PATIENTI
QUAE LIBEROS DILECTOS A CELLAE PORTA
DILIGENTER DEPELLEBAT

Preface

THE PRESENT volume was at first designed to make available to students of literature some critically significant discoveries of recent philosophy, with regard specifically to the theory of value; and that purpose still underlies the last four of the eleven chapters. When, however, after completing my reading in value theory, I returned to practical criticism to check my conclusions and find illustrations of basic principles, I was at once perplexed by a second set of problems. For one thing, critics were content, more often than I had supposed, to analyze without evaluating. For another, they sometimes made such excessive and contradictory claims for favorite analytical methods that I began to suspect a widespread misapprehension of either the scope or the limits of criticism. It had already become clear to me that analysis and evaluation together make up the whole critical process; so in the course of time I found myself working out a complete critical theory in which the theory of evaluation would form only one of two major parts. The theory of analysis now stands before that of evaluation, as logically prior to it; but both are preceded by certain necessary chapters of definition and general commentary.

The chief usefulness of the theory will, I hope, be that of clarification; for except in chapters 7 and 11—and to some extent in them also—I have tried rather to throw a framework around the whole range of critical possibility than to recommend special procedures. The need for clarification seemed to be strongly indicated by a confusion of mind I observed in my own undergraduate and graduate students of literature, who in their attempts to write critically appeared to be pulled in half a dozen different ways by as many instructors. Either they adopted a new critical method for each new course, usually without real understanding of why it had been urged on them, or they made floundering attempts to do several kinds of qualitatively different things at once. It must often have seemed to them that the attacks from which their essays returned bleeding had been motivated by an arbitrary and unpredictable malignancy. Any brief treatise on theory which helps to explain to students more adequately than an instructor can do in a few minutes of conference why critical faults are faults and where critical merits are to be sought will have some pedagogical value, if value of no other kind. It is probable, however, that among the instructors to whose judgment the critical papers are submitted are some who in moods of special honesty recognize arbitrariness in their discriminations among crimes, misdemeanors, and unconventional virtues; if so, to them also a general theory of criticism may be useful.

May I go further and admit frankly a suspicion that only the rare critic has made a systematic study of the craft he professes? Though not disinclined to drudgery, we teachers of literature (I will refrain from saying anything about journalistic critics) tend to rely on our intuitions to provide us with solutions to problems that can be solved only by the most rigorously logical analysis. In our subjective approach to rational problems, if not in our behavior when we have actually come to grips with them, we resemble the reporters sent to cover the first Bikini bomb test, who replied to scientists' questions about what they had seen immediately after the explosion by announcing their disappointment that the bang had not been louder. The bang made by a literary work— its aesthetic and intellectual impact—is of course quite properly a matter of intense concern to the critic. An attempt to measure the bang can profit, however, from an acquaintance with the mechanics and limitations of bang-measuring instruments as well as from a better-than-average aural sensitivity to detonations. And this acquaintance we are reluctant to acquire, since while we are acquiring it our attention will have to be shifted from the object of our primary interest. Accordingly we assure ourselves (to try another metaphor) that in the realm of art our way can be better felt than searched out on maps, not wishing to admit that if we are actually going somewhere we can both save time and safeguard our progress toward the destination by using maps to discover the general area in which our intuitive sense of direction can be given play.

One of the assumptions underlying the following pages, then, is that theory is not necessarily frivolous and impractical. On the contrary, it is the grammar of practice. If some persons, and those not the least talented, are confused and distracted by grammar, others are freed by it from the necessity of copying their teachers by rote. In a society in which cultural forms are rigidly authoritarian there is perhaps good reason to insist on imitation. In a democratic society like our own, however, values are perceived in new discoveries; and the most far-reaching discoveries are likely to be made by persons who know, and do not fear to claim, the full extent of their legitimate freedom.

I wish to express my gratitude to Gordon McKenzie and James Lynch, both of the University of California, and to Bertram Jessup, of the University of Oregon, for reading all or parts of the manuscript and making friendly comments and suggestions. My thanks are due also to a number of persons and publishers for permission to quote copyrighted materials, as follows: to R. P. Blackmur, author of *The Double Agent* (New York, Arrow Editions, 1935; soon to be reissued by Harcourt, Brace and Co.); to Jonathan Cape, Ltd., publishers of *The Craft of Fiction* (New York, 1931), by Percy Lubbock; to Thomas Y. Crowell Company, publishers of *Aesthetic Analysis* (New York, 1936), by D. W. Prall; to Harcourt, Brace and Company, publishers of *Theory of Literature* (New York, 1949), by René Wellek and Austin Warren, also of *Creative Criticism and Other Essays* (New York, 1931), by J. E. Spingarn; to International Publishers Company, Inc., publishers of *Social Roots of the Arts* (New York, 1949), by Louis Harap; to Thomas Munro, editor of *The Journal of Aesthetics and Art Criticism;* to John Crowe Ransom, editor of *The Kenyon Review;* to Alfred A. Knopf, Inc., publishers of *The Armed Vision: A Study in the Methods of Modern Literary Criticism* (New York, 1948), by Stanley Edgar Hyman, also of *Aspects of Literature* (New York, 1920), by J. M. Murry; to the Macmillan Company, publishers of *Criticism in the Making* (New York, 1929), by Louis Cazamian; to Oliver and Boyd, publishers of *New Literary Values: Studies in Modern Literature* (Edinburgh and London, 1936), by David Daiches; to Charles Scribner's Sons, publishers of *Criticism* (New York, 1914), by W. C. Brownell; to Joseph Shipley, editor of *Dictionary of World Literature* (The Philosophical Library, Inc., New York, 1943); to Société d'Edition "Les Belles Lettres," publishers of *Tendances nouvelles en histoire littéraire* (Paris, 1930), by Philippe Van Tieghem; and, finally, to Harvard University Press, present holders of the copyright on *General Theory of Value* (Longmans, Green and Co., New York, 1926), by Ralph Barton Perry—a work reissued in 1950 under the new imprint.

WAYNE SHUMAKER

Berkeley, California
April 4, 1952

Contents

SOCRATES: *I am myself a great lover of these processes of division and generalization; they help me to speak and to think.*

PLATO, *Phaedrus*

1

What Is Literary Criticism?

WHAT IS literary criticism? The question must be answered in order that we may know what body of subject matter we are to examine; it must be answered carefully, since what is to be discovered will depend mainly on where we decide to look. Preliminary definitions are very important indeed: by limiting the field of inquiry they not only rule out certain possible conclusions but also, in the long run, impose others. If our hope is rather to learn than to urge, the definition must accordingly be broad enough to include all the writings which are regularly, or even frequently, spoken of as critical. It must be, so to speak, a sufficiently large house to receive all the applicants for accommodations who come bearing respectable references.

Surprisingly, not many of the rather large number of persons who have written about criticism have taken the trouble to explain what the word means. They have seldom needed to do so, for their object has nearly always been to analyze less than the whole body of critical writings or to recommend certain complexes of assumptions and procedures. The situation of the general theorist of criticism, as opposed to the theorist whose views are selective, is like that in which Ralph Barton Perry found himself when he began the composition of his *General Theory of Value*. There had been, he complained, much discussion of values, but very little of value. The attempt had been to adjudicate between rival values, or to work out comparative scales, or to inquire into the nature of the Highest Good, not to discover what "value" always and everywhere meant. In the same way one can find any number of criticisms but almost no criticism. Criticism ought to do this, its proper function is that; but what it generically *is* we are hardly anywhere adequately told. Even when an "is" stands between the noun and the description, an "ought" is often thinly disguised by it, as, for instance, in Arnold's famous pronouncement that criticism is the disinterested endeavor to know and propagate the best that has been known and thought in the world.

It seems reasonable to begin the search for an unprejudiced definition in works that profess impartiality—dictionaries, encyclopedias, handbooks to literature, and the like. Quite by chance, the etymology one finds in any good dictionary by running "criticism" back to "critic" leads directly to the only real crux. Etymologies sometimes give rise to strange arguments, like Quiller-Couch's objection to "in case" on the plea that one might hunt in vain for a similar use of the Latin *casus*. Here, however, there is no irrelevance. The Greek *krinein* means "to judge or discern"; and the longer one puzzles over the central and invariable meaning of criticism the more keenly one becomes aware that everything hinges on the propriety of the "or." Is judgment a responsibility or only a privilege? The privilege, I assume, is not to be disputed, since a vast body of historical writing agreed to be critical concerns itself with faults and beauties. But is the right to judge never to be waived? Does its existence imply an unconditional obligation?

Here, then, is the issue. To follow out in crude personifications the metaphor used in the opening paragraph, the three types of applicants for admission to the *Domus Criticorum* are Judgment, Discernment, and their offspring Discerning Judgment. The references of the last are eminently satisfactory. Judgment, in spite of rather antiquated dress and arbitrary manners (he could do with some of his boy's ingratiating plausibility), comes of an old and imposing family and will have to be given lodgings out of a decent respect for old times. But Discernment? It is true that besides having quick intuitions she

2

is often capable of rigorous logic. Yet she holds herself rather aloof from practical affairs and avoids recommending positive courses of action. She appears hardly to have preferences in literature and will sometimes talk about Paul Bunyan and Shakespeare in equally neutral tones. Worse still, it is doubtful that she has any morals. Does she not belong in more relaxed company?

Grotesque as the metaphor is, its implications are mainly right. The only really troublesome problem in defining criticism has to do with the status of discernment (or, more properly, analysis) when it is unaccompanied by a direct or implied appraisal. Must formal discussion of literature be evaluative in order to be critical? Good arguments have been advanced to support both the possible replies.

The division of opinion runs through dictionaries, encyclopedias, and handbooks. The most authoritative American dictionary, Webster's *New International,* in its second edition defines the relevant sense of criticism as "the art of judging or evaluating with knowledge and propriety the beauties and faults of works of art or literature." The monumental *New English Dictionary,* however, asserts that criticism is "the art of estimating the qualities and character of literary or artistic work; the function or work of a critic." In the accompanying quotations Dryden is cited as having written that by "criticism, as it was first instituted by Aristotle, was meant a standard of judging well," and Dowden as having declared, "The effort of criticism in our time has been . . . to see things as they are, without partiality, without obtrusion of personal liking or disliking."

The difference is paralleled in other reference works, the advantage being evidently on the side of judgment but dissident views now and then asserting themselves. Thrall and Hibbard, in a *Handbook to Literature* (1936), describe the critic as "one who estimates and passes judgment on the value and quality of the work of others." Shipley's *Dictionary of World Literature* (1943) points out that the word "criticism" has been in use only since the seventeenth century, although "the judgment it represents is recorded among the Athenians, 5th c. B.C." The definition is:

> The conscious evaluation or appreciation of a work of art, either according to the critic's personal taste or according to some accepted aesthetic ideas ... Increasingly it is stated (T. S. Eliot), as it was almost always (save among the Romantics) implied, that (I. A. Richards): "to set up as a critic is to set up as a judge of values."[1]

The 1946 edition of the *Encyclopedia Americana* is in essential agreement: "In its narrow sense, the art of criticism is confined to the study of the beauties or defects of some particular work." Yet there is a broader sense, too, in which the term "includes the establishment as well as the application of principles"—a task in which "it must be largely indebted to philosophy." The eleventh edition of the *Encyclopaedia Britannica* at first also defers to the opinion that criticism is "the art of judging the qualities and values of an aesthetic object, whether in literature or the fine arts." No sooner, however, has Edmund Gosse, the author of the article, made a respectful genuflection to appraisal than he expresses another view, which he apparently prefers. The term "has come ... to possess a secondary and specialized meaning as a published analysis of the qualities and characteristics of a work in literature or fine art." On the other side, again, Ferdinand Brunetière, in *La Grande Encyclopédie* (the French equivalent of the *Britannica*) argues strongly for the duty of judgment, although he admits the increasing importance of explication, "which may at times seem to have become in our century the whole of criticism." The fifteenth edition of *Der Grosse Brockhaus* repeats the emphasis on judgment but urges relativistic standards: "*Literary-aesthetic* [criticism] concerns itself preferably with the examination of whether a writing conforms to the material and formal laws of beauty accepted at the

4

time it was composed." The *Enciclopedia Italiana* sub-
sumes *critica letteraria* under *critica* in the general sense
and defines the latter as "any activity or working of the
human mind which attempts to distinguish those qualities of a given object which have value from those which
do not."[2] Finally, the American *Dictionary of Philosophy
and Psychology*, which has a special interest because it
draws upon the disciplined thought of philosophical aesthetics (not necessarily a kind of thinking which coincides
exactly with that of literary criticism), pronounces criticism to be "the appreciation or estimation of works of
art"—an activity that would seem to include the exercise
of taste and hence an avowal of preferences.

It is evident that the "authorities" who can most confidently be expected to show impartiality are not in complete agreement. The widespread practice of critical
evaluation is admitted, but there is dissension about
whether the practice is compulsive. The reason, I think,
is fairly clear: a traditional view has lately begun to en-
counter strong opposition. The opposition is implied in
the argumentative tone of some of the definitions and
explicitly mentioned in others. The prestige of the tradition is especially apparent in Gosse's willingness to defer
to it before remarking on the emergence of a new emphasis, and the threat of the new emphasis in Brunetière's
insistence that it is improper.

It remains only to see whether good arguments have
been urged on behalf of the minority opinion. The responsibility of the general theorist of criticism is here
quite different from that of the theorist with a specific
program to recommend. Whereas the latter may resolve
any controversy to suit his convenience, the former must
be at pains, especially in the early stages of his inquiry,
not to anticipate agreements that have not yet come into
being. So far as possible, he must state generalizations
that bracket contradictory opinions without denying the
validity of any that have respectable support. To take
sides is to acknowledge partiality and exclusiveness.

Some respectable support has already been presented for the view that the critic may analyze without appraising. Much more is available. First of all there are ambiguous statements which may be interpreted either as supporting or as denying the necessity of appraising. Thus A. Ricardou asserts that "literary criticism consists in analyzing a writer's work, explaining it by its causes, judging its aesthetic value."[3] Are the three aims concurrent or separable? W. C. Brownell, on a single page if not quite in a single sentence, throws his reader into a similar perplexity. Criticism is "the statement of the concrete in terms of the abstract," its function being "to discern and characterize the abstract qualities informing the concrete expression of the artist." Its "concern," however, is "to measure [the author's] success by the correspondence of his expression to the idea it suggests and by the value of the idea itself."[4] Why need the critic be concerned about doing something which is no part of his function? Remarks like these can be cited either to support or to attack a belief that judging is an unconditional obligation.

Much more persuasive, because less quibbling, is evidence drawn from outright self-contradictions in the writings of persons who have insisted on evaluation. J. M. Murry declared unequivocally for the traditional view in one essay, only to show an inconsistent liberality in another printed in the same volume. In "The Function of Criticism" he says,

> The critic has not merely the right, but the duty, to judge between Homer and Shakespeare, between Dante and Milton, between Cezanne and Michelangelo, Beethoven and Mozart. . . . The function of true criticism is to establish a definite hierarchy among the great artists of the past, as well as to test the production of the present.

This on page 14. Yet on page 180 he admits the existence of another "important type of criticism, which is analysis of poetic method, an investigation and appreciation of

6

the means by which the poet communicates his intuitive comprehension to an audience."⁵ An "important" type of criticism, even if not "true," can hardly be ruled non-existent; and acknowledgment of its actuality by a man admittedly unfriendly to it carries special conviction. T. S. Eliot, who was cited in Shipley as an exponent of the duty of judging, can also be quoted in support of the contrary view. In *The Use of Poetry and the Use of Criticism* he said,

> I assume that criticism is that department of thought which either seeks to find out what poetry is, what its use is, what desires it satisfies, why it is written and why read, or recited; or which ... assesses actual poetry. ... [There are] these two theoretical limits of criticism: at one of which we attempt to answer the question "what is poetry?" and at the other "is this a good poem?"⁶

Appraisals, then, are offered by some critics but not by all; and Eliot himself sometimes analyzes without evaluating.

The contradictions are easier to explain than the ambiguities. The writer is thrown off balance by the disparity between what he sees and what he would like to see. He offers an ideal definition which he later confesses, either explicitly or by indirection, not to have been empirical. But the ambiguities also, whether contrived to hide issues or the result of a failure to perceive them, assist one's recognition that the requirement of judgment is not agreed to be absolute.

If this were not enough, some definitions either ignore or repudiate the necessity of evaluating. For J. M. Robertson, writing in 1889 (I begin here to note dates in order to avoid giving the impression that a minority opinion is just now emerging), criticism was "only a department of inquiry entered upon from the same kind of motives as lead men to scientific research commonly so-called. These may be summed up as the impulses of curiosity and self-expression—the desire to know, and the need to express

7

notions."' The French critic Schérer had made an even sharper disavowal as early as 1861:

> Our aesthetic prefers contemplating to judging, studying to appreciating; or, if it appreciates, it does so by letting the inmost sense of a work speak and reveal itself by degrees. It puts everything in its place, finds a place for everything. It has renounced the sterile procedure which consists in opposing one form of the beautiful to another, in preferring, in excluding. It has no prejudice, does not make up its mind in advance. It believes everything, likes everything, endures everything ... It is as vast as the world, as tolerant as nature.[8]

The most elaborate case against judgment seems to have been made out, however, by Richard Moulton in the 1880's. It deserves to be looked at in some detail.

The argument appears in the long introduction to *Shakespeare as a Dramatic Artist*, a book significantly subtitled *A Popular Illustration of the Principles of Scientific Criticism*. At the moment, said Moulton, criticism only rarely aspired to scientific objectivity. "The prevailing notions of criticism are dominated by the idea of *assaying*, as if its function were to test the soundness and estimate the comparative value of literary work." Yet there are in fact "two different kinds of literary criticism, as distinct as any two things that can be called by the same name. The difference between the two may be summed up as the difference between the work of a *judge* and of an *investigator*. The one is the enquiry into what ought to be, the other the enquiry into what is." The literary judge uses evaluative terms freely and by preference; he will not hesitate, for instance, to speak of the "decay" of the later Jacobean drama. The investigator, on the contrary, "knows nothing about higher or lower, which lie outside the domain of science." His discussion of the later Jacobean drama will be based on the perception that it is a new species, qualitatively different from the drama which immediately preceded it. "If the

8

new species be an easier form of art it does not on that account lose its claim to be analysed."[8] The scientific critic, like the physicist or sociologist, does not commit himself to assertions of goodness or badness. He accepts his *donnée* as what it is and tries to comprehend it by analysis.

Moulton guards himself carefully against narrowness. He acknowledges that judicial criticism "has long been established as a favourite pursuit of highly-cultivated minds" and has justified its existence (though he is later at pains to show how frequently evaluative judgments have been reversed). Nevertheless, it enjoys an illegitimate supremacy: "The word *criticism* itself has suffered, and the methodical treatment of literature has by tacit assumption become limited in idea to the judicial method." The explanation is that "modern criticism took its rise before the importance of induction was recognised: it lags behind other branches of thought in adapting itself to inductive treatment."[10] For a long time, however, the emphasis has been shifting.

> In the conflict between judicial criticism and science the most important point is to note how the critics' own ideas of criticism are found to be gradually slipping away from them. Between the Renaissance and the present day criticism, as judged by the methods actually followed by critics, has slowly changed from the form of laying down laws to authors into the form of receiving laws from authors.[11]

Moulton's desire at once to herald the triumph of the investigators and lament the ascendancy of the judges is no doubt inconsistent. Nevertheless, his central argument is, I think, incontestable. In the classical period (except by Aristotle, who although interpreted as a law-giver worked mainly by induction) and again after the renewal of critical inquiry at the Renaissance, it was regularly assumed that the critic's function was to measure literary works against accepted canons of aesthetic, rhetorical, and moral propriety. Even after the success of inductive methods in the physical sciences had inspired the use of analogous methods in the humanities, there continued, as the result of simple inertia, to be an insistence on the compulsion to appraise. But in the meantime the older agreement on canons had disappeared, with the result that some critics continued to apply the discredited standards; others used standards which they admitted to be personal; a few, like Brunetière, who studied the laws of genres, professed to have established new standards by induction; and still others refused to appraise at all. I believe I am not mistaken when I say that the last group has become proportionately very large and now includes many highly esteemed critics, both academic and nonacademic.

Does it follow, then, that all forms of literary inquiry are equally criticism, that there is no distinction of kind between—let us say—a study of Marlowe's death and one of Yeats's imagery? Obviously not. It would probably be agreed that studies which use literary texts as means to the solution of nonliterary problems are not literary criticism, although at every point they may call for the drawing of inferences, the weighing of alternate hypotheses, and other intellectual processes which in their own way are certainly critical. An investigation of the circumstances and causes of Marlowe's death has so remote a connection with literature that it must be described as an essay in biography: this in spite of the fact that it will undoubtedly throw some light upon literature. Again, linguistic analysis is not literary criticism when its object is not the illumination of a text or the attainment of insights into the literary use of language but knowledge desired for its bearing upon some other interest or as an end in itself. The basis of differentiation here would seem to be the nature of the primary focus. It is almost impossible, however, to separate literary criticism from literary history in some of its forms. In the abstract the grounds of distinction would appear to be the stronger emphasis of literary history on interconnections, succession, and causality. Yet much literary history hints judgments of value, and much of the best criticism is richly impregnated with history. Moreover, one is often at a loss to say whether a given piece of writing—for example, Louis Cazamian's share in *A History of English Literature*—is predominantly either one or the other. Again it would appear to be the duty of the general theorist to avoid dogmatism and accept the risk of letting his definition include too much rather than too little.

The important question, after all, has been answered. If nonevaluative discussions of literature can be criticism, it will be necessary in the remainder of the present volume to reflect on a wide variety of writings about literature and not to consider only the problems involved in judging. There is of course a disadvantage in this, since the scope of the inquiry will be considerably widened. Potentially, however, the usefulness of the findings will be increased in the measure of their breadth. What might conceivably emerge is a rationale of much literary scholarship as well as of all evaluative criticism, only those investigative procedures being excluded which subordinate an interest in literature to an interest in something else. The lack of detail (one must hope) will be compensated by a gain in amplitude.

But indeed there is no choice. The narrow meaning of criticism has been repudiated again and again since Moulton's book was published. Spingarn repudiated it in 1910 in his lecture, "The New Criticism." Cazamian repudiated it in 1929 when he wrote, "All sincere reflection upon a text is criticism of a sort; and the best criticism is just that reflection carried as far as it can go."[12] R. P. Blackmur repudiated it in 1935 by saying that he understood criticism to be simply "the formal discourse of an amateur." He added, in the same essay, "Any rational approach is valid to literature and may be properly called critical which fastens at any point upon the work itself."[13] Stanley Edgar Hyman recently noted the vogue of the repudiation in the introductory chapter of his study of modern critical methods: evaluation "has largely atrophied in the serious criticism of our time."[14] Even Richards has recanted the opinion quoted by the editors of Shipley's *Dictionary* that "To set up as a critic is to set up as a judge of values." This sentence occurs in *The Principles of Literary Criticism.* But in *Coleridge on the Imagination,* which appeared early enough to have been accessible to the editors of the *Dictionary,* Richards had already expressed his maturer view that evaluation was "suasion" or a ritual of "communion" and no essential part of the critical process.[15] His own method had become that of experiment and analysis.

It is evident, then, that a general definition of criticism must be catholic, emotionally neutral, and not contrived with the purpose of recommending a favorite program. Unfortunately, neither of the only two quoted definitions which fit these conditions is precise enough to be serviceable. Blackmur's phrase, "the formal discourse of an amateur," is at once too loose and too restrictive. (Why an amateur?) Cazamian's demand for sincerity brings the critic's motives unnecessarily into question. We must be content to say that *criticism is any intelligent discussion of literature,* taking care to enjoin that "intelligent" be interpreted liberally and that literature be the focus and not merely the vehicle of the critic's interest.

This phrasing is sufficiently broad to admit both evaluative judgment and analysis in any of its myriad forms. If it irritates some readers by opening up horizons behind which they had felt cozily secure, it will avoid frustrating others by excluding from discussion processes in which they take an especially lively interest. Moreover, as we continue to reflect about the dispute, does it not suddenly become plain that the issue can be compromised? Judgment is indeed essential to criticism—but only because intelligent analysis, like intelligent evaluation, depends heavily on the exercise of judgment. We ought to have recognized from the beginning that the handling of analytical data is no less discriminatory than choices among evaluative verdicts.

Finally, since the aim of analysis is apprehension and that of evaluation is an accurate sense of value, we may add that the ultimate critical goal, whether attainable or not, is the *full, evaluated apprehension of the critical subject matter.* *

---

* I am dissatisfied with this phrase but can think of no better one with which to replace it. The central problem has to do with the nature of the thing evaluated. Does the critic evaluate the literary work itself or does he search for value within a state of mind induced by contemplation of the work? My belief is that he usually does the latter. Valuing appears (see chap. 7) to be subjective in a way that such an operation as weighing or measuring is not. When I measure the length of a desk or weigh a bagful of flour I do so by means of an instrument which is external to my mind just as the flour or desk is external. What is distinctively mental in the process is the taking in or apprehending of the resulting datum. When I evaluate a work of literature, however, I appear to make use of a computing instrument which is inside, not outside, my mind—a sense (shall we say) of liking, or prizing, or being interested, or approving. Juxtaposition of a value sense (inside the mind) and a self-existent literary work (outside the mind) is clearly impossible. What happens, of course, is that either the value sense is somehow externalized or the literary work is taken into the mind, that is, apprehended. I should not like to say that a value sense can never be successfully externalized (again see chap. 7). On the other hand, it is evident that the apprehending of a literary work is nothing else than the act of accepting it into consciousness; hence it is reasonable to suppose that the typical critical evaluation, at least, is of the apprehension of the work and not of the work itself.

2

The Receding Goal

Is THE ultimate critical goal attainable, either immediately or as a result of the coöperative endeavor of many
men over a long period of time? Can a full, evaluated
apprehension of the critical subject be finally achieved?
To this question we must next seek an answer.

No doubt the answer can be Yes, provided we are
understood to mean that any critic may after a while
exhaust his interest in a subject and believe he under-
stands it and is aware of the essential values, both positive and negative, which it holds in solution. There is a
point beyond which returns diminish so rapidly that
additional study seems frivolous. For example, Louis
Cazamian described his own method by saying that he
attempts "to understand and interpret as fully as possible
the urge of energy" that has produced a literary text;
"to live again the stages of its development, and partake
of the impulses and intentions with which it is still preg-
nant."[1] We may imagine that when he has done these
things for a poem or novel he will expect his readers to be
satisfied.

Since Cazamian is intelligent, perceptive, and well
read, it is not difficult to agree that his criticism is always
illuminating. Is it, however, exhaustive? It can appear so
only to persons who assent to his critical program and
find his use of it in a particular instance irreproachable.
And we have already observed that there is no general
agreement about a critical program. Mr. Murry will want
to know, if M. Cazamian's subject is Wordsworth, where
that poet belongs in the hierarchy of great artists, and
this M. Cazamian will probably be reluctant to tell him.
Mr. Eliot may inquire about the "uses" of the poems;

14

M. Brunetière will wish to know whether the poems conform to the laws of the relevant poetic genres; Mr. Brownell will be concerned about the correspondence of the expressions to the ideas they suggest and the values of the ideas themselves. There is almost no limit to the possible demands. M. Cazamian would need the industry of a beaver and the patience of a saint to give satisfactory answers to everybody. More important still, he would have to be convinced that he had been wrong in adopting a program; for a program is by its nature an affirmation that some aims are preëminently or uniquely worth attaining.

I do not wish to imply that M. Cazamian's interests are unusually narrow. Messrs. Murry, Eliot, Brunetière, and Brownell would be equally unable or unwilling to write critiques that were all things to all men. The truth is that the task of "exhausting" even so restricted a subject as a single poem is virtually impossible of achievement. Take, for example, the matter of sources: "The number of elements that went to the writing of one work is infinite; no reckoning of them will ever be full; those that are most essential are elusive, intangible, cannot be caught and pinned down on the page."² Thus M. Cazamian himself, upon whom I am anxious to avoid casting special obloquy. Yet sources are only one of many conceivable objects of investigation, most of which have some interest for somebody.

Already the outlook is far from encouraging. It will become more so as we proceed, until at last the situation may seem desperate. Every avenue of approach leads into a network of back streets and alleys which must be explored if the whole area is not to be very thinly and inaccurately characterized. Or, to change the metaphor slightly, "each of the methods developed by modern critics is only in a first preliminary stage of exploration." The originators of the methods have themselves found it necessary to recognize that in spite of all their exertions they have been able to do no more than scratch the surface of literature. Every method can be extended and refined almost without limit.[3]

The comment is borrowed from Stanley Edgar Hyman, whose *Armed Vision: A Study in the Methods of Modern Literary Criticism* has greatly simplified my task at this point. Hyman analyzes the procedures of a dozen of the more distinguished recent critics and then, in a concluding chapter, speculates on the ideal critic, whose work would integrate the methods of all twelve. Such a critic would make Edmund Wilson's effective use of paraphrase, Van Wyck Brook's of biography, Carolyn Spurgeon's of statistics, Christopher Caudwell's of Marxist insights, Kenneth Burke's of symbolic transformation, and so on. The formidably armed vision which rises before the reader's eye is awe-inspiring but monstrous.

To begin with a premonitory summary, Hyman's ideal critic "would extend his whole integrated method just as far as its individual component methods are capable of extension in isolation. He would, in short, do everything possible with a work of literature." But "everything" is a great deal, so much, in fact, that for a brief lyric the discussion would extend to several volumes, and for a longer work—a long poem, a play, a novel—it would be a life study.

Does the assertion seem grotesquely exaggerated? Listen to some of the ways in which the ideal and fully rounded critic would proceed in examining a poem. He would explain "what the poem is about"; in other words, he would paraphrase it, perhaps in several ways successively in order to bring out all the layers of simultaneous meaning. He would relate the poem to earlier sources and analogues, assign it to a relevant tradition, and compare it in detail with other works, both older and contemporary, inside and outside the tradition. He would subject the poem to exhaustive analysis in the light of accessible biographical information about its author: his intellect, his personality, the circumstances of his life, his amatory and family relationships, his childhood, associations, physical appearance, habits, and professional occupation. Still unsatisfied, the critic would work out assiduously the folk sources and analogues of the poem and study the degree of the poet's dependence on folk tradition, his use of folk speech in the poem's surface texture, and the poem's "deeper polarization in the patterns of timeless primitive ritual." He would interpret the poem psychoanalytically as motivated by deep wishes and fears. Now fairly launched on his project, he would relate the poem to the expressive patterns of psychotics, savages, children, and animals. He would examine its structure in terms of image clusters organized by acts of unconscious association, in terms of structure functioning as ritual, and in terms of the poem's total Gestalt configurations and their relationship to other extrapoetic configurations. He would read the poem as a social document shaped by pressures exerted by the poet's social class, his position within the class, and his occupation. He would analyze the poem in terms both of a contemporary economic system and of economic theories justifying and transcending the contemporary system. He would discuss social and political attitudes recommended by the poem, whether explicitly or by implication. After this he would . . . But it will be simpler to let Mr. Hyman speak for himself.

He would explore at the greatest length possible its diction and the relevant ambiguous possibilities of meaning and relations in the significant words; its images and symbols and all their relevant suggestions; its formal pattern or patterns and their function and effects; its formal or informal sound devices, rhythmic structure, and other musical effects; and its larger patterns of movement and organization; as well as the interrelationships of all the foregoing. He would study all the things outside the poem to which it makes reference and interpret it in their light. He would explore and categorize the key attitude that arises out of the interrelationship of the poem's content and form, note the implications of that category, and discuss the poem comparatively with contemporary and earlier literary expressions of the same category in different terms. Our ideal critic would investigate the whole problem of what the poem communicates, how, and to whom, using every available source of information to find out what it was meant to communicate; and then every technique, from introspection to the most objective laboratory testing, to find out what it actually does communicate, to differing individuals and groups at different times and under different circumstances. He would investigate the whole problem of symbolic action in the poem, what it does symbolically for the poet, what it does symbolically for the reader, what the relationship is between these two actions, and how it functions within the larger symbolic structure of the total development of the author's writing, or even larger symbolic movements, like a literary age. . . . He would place the poem in the development of the author's writing from every angle . . . , confront the problem of the circumstances under which it arose, and discuss the unique features of its style and its unique reflections of a mind and personality. Finally, on the basis of all this analysis, our ideal critic would subjectively evaluate the poem and its parts aesthetically in relation to aim, scope, and validity of aim, and degree of accomplishment, place its value in terms of comparable works by the same poet and others, estimate its present and future significance and popularity, assign praise or blame, and, if he cared to, advise the reader or writer or both about it. If he were so inclined, he could go on and discuss his data and opinions in relation to the data and opinions of other critics, ideal or not. He would then wipe his brow, take a deep breath, and tackle another poem.'

This leaves one flattened and gasping. No wonder Hyman himself remarks at the end of the ironic summary—from which I have omitted a number of parts—"Our ideal critic is of course nonsense, although perhaps useful nonsense."⁵ What, then, will be our feeling when we realize that the ideal is cobbled together from the practices of no more than a handful of modern critics, all English or American? The plan of Hyman's book, and therefore also the analytic methods and objectives of his ideal critic, is rigorously limited. No doubt his intention was to choose in such a way as to illustrate major critical tendencies; nevertheless, I suppose he would agree that modern emphases are far from being limited to a dozen. The critical goal—the full, evaluated apprehension of the critical subject—will not be achieved when twelve men, together with their small coteries of disciples, profess themselves satisfied. There remain all the other interests not represented in the group. And since the aim of the present study is not primarily to argue the merits of differing systems but to discover, in broad outline, how criticism proceeds and what are the theoretical limits of its achievement, no one system or set of systems can be declared adequate unless provision is made for the satisfaction of every curiosity.

So far, consideration has been given only to attempts to fasten upon the nature and values of a single literary text. In order to avoid complications it is usual, in theoretical discussions, to pretend that there is no other critical purpose. Actually, everyone knows that much criticism grapples with infinitely larger problems. Periodical reviewers and a few "new" critics to one side, most writers of critical books and many writers of critical essays propose to answer questions about authors, genres, conventions, compositional techniques, movements, and other matters which require the study of many primary texts instead of only one. As the field of inquiry widens, the ideal goal recedes further into the distance, until at last it is nothing more than a presence, more forgotten than felt, beyond the horizon of awareness.

There is a way out, though its cost may seem prohibitive. The goal can be made to stand still, so that we can walk up to and around it, if we are willing to locate it on solid ground and within a modest enough distance. How this can be done will be seen in the next chapter. In the meantime we must face the fact that if the critical subject has a width and depth equal to, or in excess of, those of a single creative work, no matter how brief and trivial, the ideal goal is hopelessly, eternally unattainable. No literary work can be fully apprehended and fully evaluated by the most intense, concerted, and persistent endeavor. The universe of experience, which contains all we know or ever shall know, is continuous, and no fragment of it can be cut free for separate examination unless there is preliminary agreement on a set of arbitrary points, in the aggregate forming a complete circle (a kind of dotted line along which one is instructed to cut), to mark off an area within which one can pretend that the object is self-sufficient. I should not like to predict that the logical fictions which the drawing of the circle would require will never be generally granted. At present, however, there is certainly no general willingness to grant them.

3

The Acceptance of Limitations

THERE IS a way out, I have said, if one is prepared to buy it very dear. The sacrifice entailed is in fact double. It includes, first, the recognition of a contingency in the evaluation, and second, the radical limitation of the critical subject. Explanation of the evaluative contingency must be postponed to later chapters, in which it will be necessary to confront philosophical problems now well known to students of value theory but apparently unfamiliar to most literary theorists. The second condition is related closely to what has already been said and may be looked into at once.

Obviously, criticism can be entirely successful if it proposes to attain not the ultimate goal of critical effort, the full, evaluated apprehension of works, authors, movements, genres, and so on, but only some easy way station along the road. The situation is exactly like that of the armchair adventurer who feels an urge to climb Mount Everest but decides that at present he will merely step to the window and look eastward. An eastern window is accessible; the peak of Mount Everest is not. Similarly, the critic, after reflection, may postpone his achievement of a full, evaluated apprehension of (let us say) the poetry of Gerard Manley Hopkins and for the moment attempt only to discover the proportion of Hopkins' slant rhymes to his true rhymes. A solution to this problem is conceivable. True, ideas about the "correct" pronunciations of words differ, and if anyone were deeply interested in the matter the published statistics might set off an exchange of acrid letters in the back pages of a scholarly journal. In the long run, however, it is probable that agreement would be reached and a figure accepted as reasonably accurate.[1] The modified goal would have been reached, though the ultimate one might seem no nearer than before.

All completely successful, as opposed to profound or thought-provoking, criticism is made possible by a renunciation of the peak in favor of the window. I do not mean to suggest that the view from windows is never rewarding. Obviously, there are more favorable and less favorable windows, some of which, in lamaseries that can be reached only by the fit, and then usually after exhausting effort, offer exciting glimpses of the cloud-swept summit. Of course, the peak challenges the imagination in a way that the best-situated window does not, and one may insist on coming to grips with it directly, at whatever sacrifice of security. It can even be argued that looking out of any window is qualitatively so different from struggling where the chest heaves and the body is lashed by intoxicating winds that one prefers to remain seated. The choice need not, however, be between ignominious safety and utter destruction. There is a third possibility: one may set out for accessible parts of the slope equipped with precautionary gear—compasses, ropes, alpenstocks, maps, and experienced guides—in the hope not of scaling the last pyramid but of returning to describe something of the geology, perhaps also something of the feel, of high ledges to listeners who will very likely distrust one's report.

Concrete illustrations can easily be provided. The imaginary study of Hopkins' rhymes was written by a man who stood in front of a very small window. So little was visible to him that he was able to describe it with considerable accuracy. Anyone of normal eyesight who stood in his place would see almost exactly the same thing. Matthew Arnold, on the other hand, in his essay on "The Study of Poetry" went further in the direction of voicing mere opinions than most academic critics would care to do. Figuratively speaking, he crawled out on a high and slippery ledge, the wind whistling through his mutton chops, and stared at a prospect so immense that no two observers would be likely to bring back the same report of it. Yet even in this exposed position he tried to keep his eyes turned in a single direction; all that concerned him was to bring into focus the difference between the "best" poetry and poetry that is not the best. He showed only the slightest interest in sources, made no attempt to explicate meanings, said almost nothing about conventions, traditions, or techniques. Daring as his critical purpose was, it was infinitely more modest than the purpose of arriving at a full, evaluated apprehension of any one of the poems from which he drew his illustrations. He did not, so to speak, flounder without plan toward the absolute summit, but struck out for a very high shoulder of which he believed himself to have a clear view from the start.

Most recent criticism lies somewhere between this window and that ledge, ranging from the tight but trivial dissertation at one end to such a general thesis as that advanced by Cleanth Brooks in his already moderately celebrated essay on "The Language of Paradox" near the other. As a rule, the reliability of the critique decreases as the critic moves farther from the small but stationary observation point. In compensation there is the greater sweep of the larger statements and their wider applicability. I suppose no one would urge seriously that Brooks has "proved" the language of poetry to be everywhere and always paradoxical. At most he has called attention to an unexpected paradoxical richness in the verses he has elected to cite. His essay has, however, a power of sharpening one's general awareness of poetry in a way that the discovery about Hopkins' rhymes cannot.

In thus limiting itself, criticism has done only what has been done by every other department of modern inquiry except, possibly, some branches of philosophy, and even this exception is disputable. All exact knowledge is limited knowledge—exact, we have seen, almost in proportion as it is limited. The physical scientist, for instance, disregards the surface of reality in order to concentrate his attention on problems of internal structure. But internal structure is only one aspect of reality. The visible surface of a painting, as D. W. Prall has insisted,[2] is quite as real as the molecules of canvas and pigment that compose it. The price of the physicist's knowledge is his deliberate ignoring of whatever aspects of the universal whole do not submit themselves to his instruments. And what is true of the physicist is equally true of the physician, the biologist, the logician, the mechanic, the economist. As Prall says further,

> All knowledge is from *some* point of view, and is guided not only by data found, but by interest confined to some data and not taking in other data. All knowledge neglects some things while it pays attention to other things. All attention is directed not only by some interest, but by means of some sort of conceptual scheme. It uses a limited number of terms and definitions; it comprises some single, though perhaps very spacious, perspective upon our world.

Limitation is thus preliminary to the acquisition of any knowledge at all. "It is necessary . . . to abstract from the concrete mass presented by nature's processes, some aspects of nature connected by some specific relations and thus capable of being viewed together."[3] If it is objected that "since any analysis omits at least something, as all actual thought is bound to do, it is therefore not the whole truth," the retort is waiting: "Nothing is the whole truth."[4]

Nothing is the whole truth. This is the wisdom that men have been gradually and painfully acquiring ever since Bacon exhorted them to stop wondering about final causes and discover efficient causes by observation. Critics as well as scientists have profited from the method, less spectacularly, perhaps, but still profoundly. If we know more today than the most brilliant minds of a century or two ago could know about the sources of literature, the psychological drives that motivate it, its relation to its age, and many aspects of its formal and technical patterns, the reason is that fragmentary apprehensions have been steadily accumulating. And yet, as always, in proportion as we learn more we realize that we know less. The peak of the mountain continues steadily to recede.

If I have somewhat overstated my point for the sake of emphasis, it remains broadly true that one basic difference between the serious literary criticism of the last seventy-five to one hundred years and that of earlier times is the greater modesty of recent critics, their greater willingness to struggle, often at the expense of enormous trouble, with problems that to their predecessors would have seemed trivial or contemptible.

Even a brief recapitulation of critical history will suffice to draw the contrast. Plato showed an interest in the moral effects of poetry (*The Republic*) and its psychological sources (the *Ion* and *Symposium*). It is significant, however, that Plato's interest in poetic madness grew out of his interest in ethics, whereas modern theories of inspiration as related to the subconscious mind are relatively free of evaluative implications.[5] Aristotle attempted to explain in a single concise treatise the origin, structure, and psychological effect of the whole corpus of Greek tragedy and to compare tragedy both structurally and evaluatively with the epic. Horace undertook to lay down in a brief poem all the important "rules" for the composition of verse. Longinus made a rhetorical analysis of sublimity, from which source, he declared, and from no other, the greatest writers had won their preëminence and earned immortal fame. Quintilian, Dionysius of Halicarnassus, and their medieval and Renaissance successors had a much fuller confidence that they knew everything of importance about writing than have their twentieth-century counterparts, the authors of freshman rhetorics. In the Renaissance and for some time thereafter, critics continued to address themselves to the largest conceivable questions: the "laws" of composition, the passing of final judgments on dramas and epic poems, and such theses as that supported by Sidney, that poetry is more philosophical than history and less "hard of utterance" and "mistie to bee conceived" than philosophy. As late as the nineteenth century the assumption of near omniscience persisted in certain critical backwaters. But in the meantime a new set of intellectual presuppositions had begun a steady rise toward dominance. As early as 1602, in Daniel's *Defence of Ryme,* an entire critical document was devoted to the exploration of a rather highly specialized topic; some of Dryden's criticism (for example, his "Examen of The Silent Woman" in *An Essay of Dramatic Poesy*) adumbrates, though it does not achieve, a modern limitation of scope; and finally, after astonishing successes of the method of partition and conquest in the physical sciences, responsible criticism (which must be distinguished from merely stimulating or readable criticism) began to strive more and more regularly for the attainment of partial apprehensions.

It is extremely difficult to find in our own time critical classics comparable in reputation to those that have been cited from earlier centuries. The reason is partly that we are too near recent criticism to see it in perspective and partly that the prestige of men has in large part yielded to that of methods. If arbitrary selections were to be made, however, one could hardly do better than to choose, as widely admired books which exploit major critical interests, *The Road to Xanadu,* by J. L. Lowes, and *The Craft of Fiction,* by Percy Lubbock. Lowes confined himself to a study of the sources, in Coleridge's wide miscellaneous reading, of parts of two rather brief poems; Lubbock announced that he would examine the ways in which some representative novels were "made," or put together as structural wholes. As contemporary criticism runs, Lubbock's aim was certainly venturesome. Nevertheless, the aim permitted—indeed, demanded—that he renounce an interest in nearly all the aspects of fiction which it had been traditional for critics to discuss: characters, implied attitudes toward life, ethical standards, and social milieux.

It may be said generally that the tendency of recent criticism has been to renounce more and more of its possible subject matter in order to fix its attention with greater intensity upon narrow problems. Except in popular reviews, for at least half a century the trend has been strongly toward the analysis of parts or aspects rather than of wholes. Even formal analysis, which is sometimes thought of as having to do with the totality of a poem or a novel, arrives at its insights by ignoring the outward-pointing meanings which for "untrained" readers contain the greater part of the work's values.

Since critics as well as other men may lack complete understanding of what they do, I would not wish to profess that the principles and tendencies I have described are universally recognized. Nevertheless, acknowledgments can now and then be found that favorite methods lead only to incomplete findings or that the typical critique attains unity by rejecting whatever findings have no bearing upon a chosen thesis. Thus R. P. Blackmur, in "A Critic's Job of Work," confesses that

> These approaches—these we wish to eulogise—are not the only ones, nor the only good ones, nor are they complete. No approach opens on anything except from its own point of view and in terms of its own prepossessions. . . . Every critic like every theologian and every philosopher is a casuist in spite of himself. To escape or surmount the discontinuity of knowledge [a discontinuity that is *not* paralleled in the universe of experience], each resorts to a particular heresy and makes it predominant and even omnivorous.[6]

W. C. Brownell points out that

> A work of criticism is in fact as much a thesis as its theme, and the same thematic treatment is to be expected of it. . . . We may say indeed that all criticism of moment, even impressionist criticism, has

this synthetic aspect at least, as otherwise it must lack even the appearance of that organic quality necessary to effectiveness.

When a critical writing, like the typical essay by Lowell, is "agglutinate and amorphous," it loses force[7]—an observation that will be assented to by every teacher who has graded the critical papers of undergraduates.

There is, accordingly, no occasion for wonder that even the so-called "new" critics, who seem to pride themselves on their broad perspectives and their superiority to the uninspired drudgery which is the chief claim to distinction of the average academicist, sometimes write on such topics as "Shakespeare's way of compounding latinical elements with his native English" or "Hardy's Philosophical Metaphors."[8] Critics not "new" but, as they think, in the tradition of sound critical scholarship are more likely to discuss the possibility that *Endymion* was intended as a Neoplatonic allegory, to explain why at the end of *Paradise Lost* Adam doubts whether he should repent his sin, or to examine the indebtedness of Novalis to Shakespeare—unless, indeed, they desert literature altogether and write on noncritical problems tangential to it, like Wordsworth's business transactions or Browning's knowledge of music.[9] All, however, except the lighter journalists, limit themselves to achieve a fuller and sharper responsibility. The day of the "authority" is gone, and no substitute for him has been found except a declared and constantly focused impersonal reference frame.

4

The Two Kinds of Critical Statement

WE HAVE SEEN, first, that unless criticism is to be defined preferentially, in accordance with some personal ideal of what it ought "rightly" or "properly" to be, it must be described simply as intelligent discussion of literature; second, that the critical goal—a full, evaluated apprehension of works, periods, movements, conventions, techniques, and the like—is, practically speaking, unattainable; and finally, that the necessity of limiting each critical book or essay to some part of the total critical process has been increasingly recognized in recent years. One more step must be taken before specific critical methods and practices can be surveyed. Some principle of division must be discovered, some method of classification which will permit an attack to be made on less than the whole body of subject matter at once. Divide and conquer: it was Hitler's all-too-effective military strategy; it is the Baconian principle of scientific investigation; it is the method of nearly all profitable speculation.

Unfortunately, in the realm of pure concepts the slicing of wholes into sections is difficult. A military strategist can mark off a map of Europe into squares. An entomologist can separate the life cycle of an insect into successive chronological stages. In a manner of speaking, both procedures are dictated by nature, which presents itself to the human senses partly in terms of space and time. In logic, however, spatial and temporal categories are less useful. No good purpose would be served by analyzing criticism with reference to geographical coordinates, or, since historical development is not now in question, to months or years of origin. Another favorite category of modern thought, causality, is also irrelevant to the immediate problem, which has to do with being and not with becoming. The task of finding the principle of division best suited to the end in view is consequently by no means easy.

A little thought leads to the conviction that there is no perfect and inevitable system of classification. The range of choice is almost illimitable.

For example, the editors of Shipley's *Dictionary of World Literature* elected to classify criticism according to function. There is criticism to justify and explain one's own practice (Boccaccio, Tasso, Dante, Dryden, Hugo, Wordsworth, Eliot); criticism to justify imaginative literature (medieval and Renaissance criticism generally); prescription for writers and legislation for the taste of the multitude (Horace, Scaliger, Marxist critics, Jeffrey); criticism as a service to writers and criticism as a service to the public (Horace, Vida, Boileau, Pope, Sainte-Beuve, Arnold, Auden). Eliot has drawn a simpler distinction: there are historical, philosophic, and literary criticisms, of which the third is most "genuine."[1] A London *Times* reviewer remarked not long ago on the differences of macroscopic, microscopic, and middle-distance criticism, citing C. M. Bowra as a writer of the first, Cleanth Brooks as a writer of the second, and Geoffrey Grigson as a writer of the third.[2] Louis Cazamian opposed "History, the erudite knowledge of the conditions, the circumstances, the relations—in a word, the externals—of literature" to "the impressionism of direct, concrete perceptions."[3] J. M. Robertson pointed out that criticism may be concerned with "the objective purport" of literature, "the subjective purport" (what the work reveals of the writer's mind), and "the medium" (the style—the charm or merit of the language).[4] The editors of a recent anthology of critical essays have arranged their materials under the headings "Source," "Form," and "End."[5] Stanley Edgar Hyman adopted a classification based on critical method, but went to some pains to indicate his awareness that the choice was arbitrary. A classification might have been made by focus: Blackmur would then be called a specialist in words, Miss Spurgeon a specialist in images, Empson a specialist in forms, Burke a specialist in the totality of an author's work, and so on. Or groupings could have been worked out in accordance with the kinds of learning brought to bear on the critical problems. Eliot would then be the critic who knows literature that has passed temporarily out of fashion, Van Wyck Brooks the critic who knows minor writers, Caudwell the critic who knows modern science, and Miss Bodkin the critic who knows the classics. Again, the classification might have been by attribute. Empson would then be the keen reader, Burke the coruscating intelligence, Richards the patient teacher, Blackmur and Miss Spurgeon, in different ways, the deliberate and painstaking workers.[*]

There is hardly any end to possible sets of categories. I shall be badly mistaken if some readers of the preceding paragraph did not contrive, as they read, other sets of categories that seemed to them more useful (I hope they did not think more "truthful") than any of those mentioned. The fact is that criticism has many aspects, any one of which can be made central in analysis. It is not more "correct" to examine the critical process with reference to function than with reference to focus, or with reference to focus than with reference to means. Descriptive adjectives capable of differentiating criticisms might be multiplied indefinitely: textual, judicial, appreciative, interpretive, rhetorical, historical, linguistic, biographical, psychological, philosophical, aesthetic, comparative, personal, impersonal, romantic, realistic, classical, common-sense, liberal, conservative, reactionary, technical, statistical, formal, material, factual, imaginative, and so on endlessly.

Thus it becomes evident that logical analysis of the kind we are attempting requires, first, a clearly conceived and frankly stated purpose, and second, the adoption of analytic procedures which are suitable for the achievement of the purpose. A third desideratum, less important but still highly valuable, is simplicity. The Copernican astronomy replaced the Ptolemaic not because it is true that the sun is stationary but because the movements of solar bodies can be described more easily if the sun instead of the earth is used as a reference point.

The purpose of the present volume is to arrive at a general or large-scale understanding of the nature and methods of *all* criticism. The point of view in the remaining chapters will be that of an observer who moves gradually closer to his materials from a preliminary position high enough to reveal them all in simultaneous panorama—for the sake of an image, let us say that of a balloonist who from time to time lowers himself to a new vantage point but never drops so near his object as to be able to see its finer details. Our interest is in the entire panoply of critical possibility, not, except secondarily and by derivation, in origins, trends, personalities, and all the other matters which engage the attention of the historian.

It must be admitted at once that balloonists have widely varying perceptions from identical heights. One observer may have an eye especially for densely settled areas, another for open spaces, a third for mountains, a fourth for river courses; moreover, the physical organs of observation, the eyes, vary from keen to myopic and have special organic peculiarities, such as astigmatisms along different axes. It is therefore useless to hope that all descriptions of the panorama will coincide. The most that can be expected is that the observer's referents be specified and the report he makes in terms of them be reasonably complete.

But is it possible that any description of so huge a prospect can be reasonably complete even in terms of a limited number of referents? The answer is Yes, provided one takes care to distinguish between positive and negative qualities, and resists the temptation to select as determinants two positive qualities which between them do not characterize all the materials to be analyzed. In other words, pairs of dichotomous terms, if exactly dichotomous, will cover the entire field to which they have reference; but sets of more than two terms are almost certain to leave parts of the field uncharacterized.

It may have been noticed that several of the categorial systems mentioned just now consisted of three elements. Historical, philosophical, literary; macroscopic, microscopic, and middle-distance; subjective purport, objective purport, medium; source, form, end: evidently there is a strong natural tendency to formulate logical problems in conceptual triads. One reason may be that when the analyst has contrasted a pair of roughly opposite qualities he notes that there is a remainder, which he then tries to describe by a third term. Unfortunately, the remainder is often so indiscriminate in character that part of it escapes the bearing of the third term and disappears from the subsequent analysis. If fourth and fifth terms are added there is usually again a remainder, but at some point it seems necessary to stop subdividing and make use of the classes. In general, odd as the principle may sound, the remainder often tends to be less in proportion as the analytic terms are fewer; and it disappears entirely when only two truly dichotomous terms are utilized.

The method of simple division, as analysis by dichotomies is sometimes called, has for our purpose the tremendous advantage of preventing the omission of any of the materials we propose to study. Thus a classification of trees as deciduous or nondeciduous provides room for every conceivable tree, known or unknown, since all trees must either shed or retain their leaves in winter. The metasequoia or dawn redwood, when discovered recently in a remote part of China, proved to be deciduous, and thus fitted readily into one of two pre-existent categories. On the other hand, a classification of vertebrate animals as having two or four legs would fail

33

to include animals of three or eight legs if any were found to exist. If an attempt were made to guard against this contingency by increasing the number of classes to one hundred, vertebrates with any number of legs up to one hundred would be accommodated, but seals, which have appendages at once like and unlike legs, would cause embarrassment, and fish, which have appendages that hardly resemble legs at all, would fall outside all the classes. From the point of view of comprehensiveness, the method of simple division is accordingly much the safest for the analyst to adopt.

Obviously, the pair of terms chosen must be truly dichotomous and not merely opposites. "Good" and "bad," for instance, stand at opposite ends of a continuum instead of describing the two halves of a line. To the ethical theorist it would appear transparently false to say that all human actions are either good or bad. Many actions, perhaps most, are morally neutral. If the third term "neutral" is added to the original two, the resulting triadic system is adequately comprehensive. The reason is not, however, that the argument in favor of dichotomies was delusive. Two acts of division were performed instead of one: human actions were first separated into two classes, those having and those not having ethical color, and the former class then broken into two parts, one consisting of "good" actions (those having positive ethical value), the other of "bad" actions (those having negative value).

When measured against this procedural standard, every one of the classifications of criticism cited earlier shows itself to be unsatisfactory.[7] What is wanted is the simplest kind of preliminary categories—categories which can be subdivided later, but which from the very beginning will permit the assignment of every possible assertion about literature to one or the other of two qualitatively different types. We hope to break criticism clean in two like a biscuit, so that any part of it which is not in one half will necessarily be in the other.

34

The cleavage implicit in the first chapter and to a lesser extent in the second and third—a cleavage, moreover, which has been recognized by a number of theorists as implicit in the materials and one which will immensely clarify one of the central problems to be confronted later—is that between evaluative and nonevaluative statements. The difference is not of function, method, focus, or attribute but of logical status, although initially it may announce itself to the perceptions as something else.

A person sensitive to emotional nuances may sometimes feel the logical distinction between a judgment and a description or characterization (for a purely analytical assertion is nothing else) as a contrast of tone. Thus the meteorological report of a sudden shower given in a radio newscast sounds different from the comment of a disgusted tennis player. The former is emotionally neutral; the latter is not. There is a similar though less obvious tonal contrast between the assertion that Whitman's poetry is egotistical and the observation that few or none of the poems contain bookish allusions. A subjective means of differentiation is not, however, one that can be confidently handled, and discrimination is often complicated by the admixture of analysis and appraisal in single sentences and by the effort of some critics to throw all their remarks into a single mood—enthusiastic, denunciatory, judicious, or whatever.

We shall do well, therefore, to discriminate on logical grounds and disregard differences of tone. And indeed, the logical contrast is much the sharper of the two. A full explanation of the differing logical status of judgments and analyses must be postponed to chapters 8 and 9; at present I can only say, with some appearance of dogmatism, that whereas nonevaluative statements can be verified, within some degree of probability, by reference to the object and perhaps also its milieu, judgments of value must be tested by reference also to an evaluative assumption wholly independent of the object. The assertion that a poem contains the property x, or a stated degree or quantity of x, can be tested, once the nature of x is understood, by an examination of the poem; but the claim that because x is present the poem has value rests on a proposition external to the work (that all poems which contain x have value). The double reference of evaluative statements sets them apart from statements which have no evaluative implications and hence lack the same basic contingency.

If the foregoing summary is too compact to be intelligible, I must beg the reader's indulgence for a time or ask him to turn at once to the chapters in which the full explanation is offered. In the meantime I can perhaps suggest the drift of the complete argument by a visual image. In studying criticism we are moving in a world which consists of a ground, and objects at various distances above the ground. The ground represents the literature being criticized; the objects above it represent the assertions made about the literature. Some of the objects are supported from beneath by blocks or pillars; these are the purely analytic (nonevaluative) assertions. The rest are supported from above, by suspension from structures which may or may not be in sight, but which do not rest on the visible ground. These are the evaluative assertions. Close examination reveals that the difference between the two classes of objects, which appears to the sensitive but unanalytic observer as one of undefined or only partly definable (tonal) quality, results from their contrasting means of support.

Our preliminary dichotomy, then, is between evaluative critical statements, on the one hand, and analytic or descriptive (nonevaluative) statements, on the other. The categories are not only empirically useful but also logically exhaustive. No critical statement which is neither evaluative nor nonevaluative can be imagined. If there can sometimes be found, in a critical book or essay, a sentence or paragraph which neither immediately nor prospectively characterizes or passes judgment

36

on a literary subject, it will be discovered not really to discuss literature at all. It consequently falls outside the terms of the definition given in chapter 1, and does not require attention as criticism.

One caution must be added. A single sentence may contain both a description and an evaluation. The assertion that Arthur Miller's *Death of a Salesman* does not elevate and exhilarate, and therefore is not good tragedy, at once characterizes and appraises and hence must be examined in two separate contexts. Such a fracturing of critical documents is in some respects awkward. One must take comfort in the realization that analysis is always disruptive and in the hope that compensation may be found in a clearer understanding of the fundamental nature of the critical process.

The analytical part of criticism will be discussed in the following three chapters; the evaluative part, which presents more puzzling logical problems, in the final four.

5

Analysis: External Reference Frames

IT WAS SEEN in chapter 3 that "All knowledge is from *some* point of view, and is guided not only by data found, but by interest confined to some data and not taking in other data. . . . All attention is directed not only by some interest, but by means of some sort of conceptual scheme. It uses a limited number of terms and definitions; it comprises some single, though perhaps very spacious, perspective upon our world." We must accordingly seek a classification of analytical perspectives, hoping once again to find a natural dichotomy that will insure completeness.

The most useful division is between criticism which attempts to bring to literature insights found outside its perimeter, and criticism which dives directly to the center of the literature and works outward to the perimeter. The difference was considered at length by R. G. Moulton in 1915, and has recently been made familiar to both practicing critics and literary theorists by its functional importance in the structure of René Wellek's and Austin Warren's *Theory of Literature,* a volume which has had a wide sale in academic circles and in some universities has become the subject of heated controversy.

Moulton's explanation of the difference turned on the words "outer" and "inner." Criticism which proceeded from without inward he called "outer" study; that which remained inside the critical subject he called "inner" study. His own preference was strongly for "inner" study, since he believed that "outer" study refused recognition to precisely the aspect of literature which most deserved attention, the laws of its essential being. There was an analogy with pure and applied mathematics; but whereas applied mathematics was a development of the pure science, "literature is in the difficult position that the multifarious applications have first established themselves, and the pure study has, with difficulty, to be disentangled from them."[3]

Wellek and Warren are less frankly partisan. "The most widespread and flourishing methods of studying literature," they say in introducing a series of chapters on "extrinsic" and "intrinsic" critical approaches, "concern themselves with its setting, its environment, its external causes . . . Nobody can deny that much light has been thrown on literature by a proper knowledge of the conditions under which it has been produced; the exegetical value of such a study seems indubitable."[4] Yet they too clearly prefer intrinsic study: "The natural and sensible starting point for work in literary scholarship is the interpretation and analysis of the works of literature themselves. After all, only the works themselves justify all our interest in the life of an author, in his social environment and the whole process of literature."[5]

Although we cannot try now to adjudicate between the two rival procedures, it is proper to observe that one of the central issues of critical theory is that of the relative usefulness of external and internal reference frames. Dialectically, the "new" critics, who like to believe that they discuss literature in terms of itself, are more agile than the conservatives, who put a high value on the comparative certainty attainable by the use of external data. In consequence, the conservatives are sometimes reduced to the necessity of posing as thick-witted, insensitive plodders who are regrettably unable to follow the transcendental speculations of their opponents.[6] Nevertheless, the pages of scholarly journals continue to be filled, for the most part, with studies that depend frankly on external reference frames. The reason is not far to seek. However eagerly literature may aspire to absolute self-existence, it arises in an extraliterary milieu that dictates the modes of consciousness in which it is conceived.

39

The milieu itself may be studied and the findings applied to the literature the critic wishes to apprehend.

The usefulness of external reference frames is accordingly beyond question. Critics whose personal commitments are to intrinsic study have often found it necessary to admit the relevance of data obtained by extrinsic approaches. Thus F. R. Leavis speaks of "the inevitableness with which serious literary studies lead outside themselves, and of the cogency with which they ask to be associated with studies outside the strictly literary-critical field."' "No one," says Louis Cazamian of philological and historical methods, "will seriously dispute their claims in their proper spheres . . . No doubt, the growth of literature in time comes within the wide domain of the science of the human past; and a sound knowledge of the facts of development is the foundation for all critical endeavor."' No adequate grounds for the rejection of such considerations are likely to be discovered. If by full apprehension is meant, among other things, an understanding of literature as it was intended by its authors and interpreted by contemporary readers, research beyond the limits of individual works is no more avoidable than a historian's interest in the origin and function of a social institution which has aroused an intrinsic interest.

The chief difficulty in handling the distinction is in recognizing where one kind of study blends into the other. For example, is Aristotle's *Poetics* extrinsic or intrinsic criticism? Intrinsic, most persons would probably reply; yet many of Aristotle's comments are traceable to a formistic assumption that there is an ideal tragic form toward which all actual tragedies strive. This assumption he probably brought to his reading of the dramas, as in sections having to do with catharsis he spoke in terms which had reference to ethics and medicine. In a similar way every critic sees his primary documents through eyes modified by individual experience and a group heritage.

Is it, then, accurate to say that any criticism is completely "inner"? Evidently not; but it can be understood that "outer" study, or the use of an extrinsic approach, or analysis by means of an external reference frame (I use the terms synonymously), aims at the illumination of literature by an exploration primarily of "its setting, its environment, its external causes," whereas "inner" study, or an intrinsic approach, or analysis by means of an internal reference frame, restricts itself as consistently as possible to a turning over of what can be found within the literary object itself. The critic's perspective may, of course, be sufficiently "spacious" to admit to the same essay findings obtained by both intrinsic and extrinsic approaches;[9] but for our purpose criticism which utilizes both methods must be divided and its parts considered separately.

In the remainder of the present chapter we shall look briefly at external frames; in the next we shall examine internal frames.

Once again it will be necessary to arrive at our own subdivisions. The most careful attempt to specify the varieties of extraliterary knowledge which can be brought to bear on a literary subject seems to have been made by Wellek and Warren, who include under the heading "The Extrinsic Approach to the Study of Literature" chapters on the relation of literature to biography, psychology, society, ideas, and the other arts.[10] These groupings suggest the classification to which any inductive study of extrinsic criticism would probably lead; but since the purpose of the present volume is less to discover trends than to envisage (and examine) possibilities, we must again try to achieve a fuller coverage by dichotomizing.

The context in which literature is placed by the extrinsic critic may be the events and psychic states of the writer's life or one or more aspects of the composite life of a cultural group in which the writer is included. Again, it may be the events and ideas of another age than the writer's; or it may be a conceptual system which is

41

thought to be eternally true and therefore to lie outside human time. In other words, we may separate external reference frames first into contemporary and noncontemporary, and then subdivide the latter into temporally distant and atemporal.

Each writer differs in significant ways from his contemporaries. So far as his writings express his individuality rather than his communally shared experiences, a study of his life will increase our comprehension of his works. The relevant part of the life may be an outward event or chain of events. It has often been thought, for example, that Milton's desertion by his first wife—a concrete and datable happening—was directly responsible for his writing of a series of divorce tracts, and indirectly responsible for the tone of certain passages in his poetry. Or some attitude or idea expressed by a writer may awaken curiosity about his intellectual or emotional history (which is affected by outward events, but may be conceived of as distinct from them). Why did Milton say in his sixth Latin elegy that aspiring young poets ought to preserve their chastity and drink pure water from beechen bowls? The search for a reply, if pushed far enough, would lead into the history of ideas, but it can be cut short at the detection of similar notions in Milton's reading (this is the technique of the source hunter) or at the reconstruction of a home or school atmosphere capable of producing a yearning for austere self-dedication (this is the method of the psychographer).

Such problems are genetic; but, contrary to the assumption of many theorists that all extraliterary research aims at the establishment of causal relationships, biographical data can be used to interpret obscure passages in texts. What horrible crime provoked the remorse of Byron's Manfred? A solution cannot be found on the printed page; therefore it has been sought in the circumstances of the author's banishment from England. The interpretation of doubtful passages in the light of biographical information is in fact by no means uncommon.

The word "spare" in Milton's twentieth sonnet, said W. J. Rolfe, "is, on the face of it, ambiguous; but no one who knows Milton as a man ought to misinterpret it."[11]

Again, every writer is similar in significant ways to his contemporaries. Understanding of his writings can accordingly often be enriched by the study of group history in any of its numerous forms—political, economic, social, intellectual, and so on.

The bearing of political history on literature, although perhaps less evident than that of social and intellectual history (which determine basic modes of consciousness), can be abundantly illustrated. Bale's *Kyng Johan*, Norton and Sackville's *Gorboduc*, and Addison's *Cato* were dramas motivated partly or wholly by contemporary political situations, hence dramas which point outward to an environment. Novels by Disraeli, Trollope, and many other writers have political settings which may not be immediately familiar to readers of another country and age. Poems like Dryden's "Absalom and Achitophel," Shelley's "The Mask of Anarchy," and Wordsworth's "To Toussaint l'Ouverture" are hardly meaningful without some knowledge of political history. Huge numbers of speeches, pamphlets, and the like, including works as unmistakably literary as Milton's *Areopagitica* and Burke's *Reflections on the Revolution in France*, are made of the very stuff of politics. Even critics whose interest in literature is purely belletristic often find that the sketching in of the political background is a necessary preliminary to the internal criticism of such works. Neither is "great" literature always more fully independent of politics than a comparatively trivial poem like the Toussaint sonnet. Spenser's *Faerie Queene* contains a political allegory; large numbers of political allusions have been discovered, or suspected, in Shakespeare's plays; many epics, among them Virgil's *Aeneid*, have political overtones; and Dante's *Divine Comedy* is so steeped in contemporary politics that only specialists can read it without a commentary. The price of ignoring political settings, here and elsewhere, is limited comprehension.

What has been said of politics could be repeated with only slight changes of wording about economics, sociology, the history of ideas, and all the other studies which help toward a comprehension of the ultraindividual forces that exert pressure on literature. The critic of *The Deserted Village* may legitimately wish to know whether Goldsmith's description of the impact of industrialism on agricultural communities is overdrawn. Crabbe's poetry will suggest questions for which replies must be sought in historical sociology. The lover of Keats may become interested in structural techniques inspired by the current associational psychology. One can hardly imagine a limit to the varieties of curiosity that literature may stimulate. The student of Homer may be glad to avail himself of Gilbert Murray's discussions of military tactics at the time of the Trojan War. The specialist in Elizabethan drama may become absorbed in reflections about the catering of playwrights to a rising middle class. The reader of Arthur Koestler's *Arrival and Departure* may appreciate an expert opinion about the author's competence in psychoanalysis. An inquisitiveness about form or craftsmanship (usually thought to be characteristic of the inner critic) often motivates research in contemporary rhetoric or aesthetics. The analysis of a work's place in literary history or of the degree and nature of a writer's originality requires the constant drawing of lines outward from the central critical subject.

Enough has been said to make clear that no work of literature exists in a vacuum, and that an effort to apprehend it fully can lead—I speak without exaggeration—anywhere within the contemporary environment. As Edwin Greenlaw has said,

> The influence of the time . . . is unconscious and inescapable. It limits while it defines the transcript of life which major poetry gives us. Thus poetry is not merely verse, or music, or high imagination, or

44

dream and fantasy, but reality ... It is distilled and concentrated experience.[12]

Not even a puristic preoccupation with the aesthetic surface is capable of restricting attention wholly to design.

> The more concretely we examine form, the more we become involved in content. The farther we get from content, the more abstract the consideration of form becomes. The analysis of the form of tragedy in general may be highly abstract, but work with the structure of *Hamlet* or any specific play is saturated with content. The organic unity of form and content is the concrete work of art.[13]

Thus a recent Marxist critic whose chief interest is the social origin of content. It is rarely indeed that an intention to discuss literature in terms of itself does not at some point yield to the necessity of recognizing the pressure of an external context.

Noncontemporary frames can be dismissed more briefly, since a widely diffused historical relativism has had a powerful impact on recent critical methodologies. Nevertheless, a given work may invite—may, indeed, dictatorially enjoin—examination of the ideas or happenings of another age. "The fabric of the play," wrote Dryden in the preface to *All for Love*, "is regular enough ... and the unities of time, place, and action, more exactly observed, than perhaps the English theatre requires." For once Dryden attempted to observe the dramatic "rules"; and since the rules were professedly drawn from Aristotle, the critic of *All for Love* may not think his responsibilities exhausted if he has not briefly inquired whether observation of the rules sufficed to produce a truly Aristotelian play. French drama of the classical period suggests a similar analysis, as do also, less imperatively, some of Ben Jonson's plays. Historical novels, again, by their inner nature direct attention to a temporally distant reference frame. Was Scott's knowledge of the Middle Ages accurate? Did Thackeray imitate the Augustan style effectively in *Henry Esmond*? How trustworthy is the

Roman setting described by Robert Graves in *I, Claudius*? As often as literature is retrospective it provokes questions like these; and it is often retrospective.

Less frequently a critic is struck by accidental similarities between works remote from each other in time. *The Golden Ass* of Lucius Apuleius may be shown to have much in common with eighteenth-century picaresque novels, or Bunyan's *Grace Abounding* to have a significant resemblance to St. Augustine's *Confessions*. Or an author may be said to have been born out of his time, to belong properly in a remote place and age—as it might be said (with how much point is not now in question) that Matthew Arnold had a Greek mind and Cardinal Newman a medieval one. The opportunities for juxtapositions of this kind are almost limitless. No doubt it is possible that a noncontemporary frame may be chosen unwisely. For instance, it would seem unprofitable to analyze President Truman's speeches by reference to a Quintilian rhetoric, though some findings would no doubt emerge. Yet noncontemporary frames, like contemporary ones, have valid uses and sometimes both broaden and deepen an understanding of inherent literary qualities.

Impressionistic criticism uses a noncontemporary frame whenever the literary subject is not of very recent origin. The frame is here the impressionist's sensibilities, upon which a given work is said to have certain effects; and if the work and the critic are appreciably separated by time, the two poles of the analysis are necessarily noncontemporary.

There remain only atemporal frames: those which underplay the dynamics of literature in favor of the statics. Any deeply held conviction about what literature ought always and everywhere to be is likely to motivate analysis in the light of eternal principles. The principles may be philosophical, aesthetic, moral, or of almost any other conceivable kind. Plato's analysis of Homer in the tenth book of *The Republic* arrived at the earlier of two damning conclusions ("the imitator has no knowledge worth mentioning of what he imitates") because it was guided by convictions about the nature of ultimate reality. A formistic aesthetic leads to inquiries about the observance of rules appropriate to a genre. Ethical preoccupations may dictate an analytic approach, as in Ruskin, who not only insisted on truthfulness (that is, faithful representation of the external surface of experience) but also wished to find in literature, as in art generally, attributes which he posited of the Deity—unity, repose, symmetry, and so on.[14] The critic whose analyses are motivated by these or similar convictions can often move easily from analysis to evaluation. At present, however, we are concerned only with analysis; and enough has been said to indicate the possibility that the external reference frame may be so conceived as to lie outside historical time. It is evident, indeed, that all evaluative assumptions other than relativistic ones belong here: they inspire a search for eternally precious qualities.

These, then, are illustrations of the large orders of external analytic frames. I have done no more than suggest the enormous variety of ways in which the apprehension of literature can benefit from scrutiny in the light of knowledge obtained elsewhere than in the literature itself. The reader can fill in the outline at will; I have wished only to sketch a framework.

It must be noted in conclusion that the external frame of reference may sometimes so engross attention that it usurps centrality and the literary subject becomes secondary. When this occurs the writing ceases to be "critical" in the sense used in these pages; its relation to literature—to borrow a comparison of Blackmur's—becomes that of the chemistry of ivory to a game of chess.[15] But the focus can be kept unblurred, and every loop made outside the literary subject can bring the critic back home with his eyes sharpened and his interest undiminished. If he returns so, his journey of discovery has found justification.

6

Analysis: Internal Reference Frames

IN THE last thirty or forty years it has often been keenly felt, and sometimes bitterly argued, that a loop outside the literary subject does not always lead back inside the perimeter; that the professional student's eyes become sharpened for the wrong kind of data and his interest in literature shrinks to the point of disappearance. Too many journeys of discovery (it is alleged) end in foreign ports, where the hard-won gold is squandered without increase of the domestic riches. Let us patronize our home industries. Let us "See Literature First," visit its own Yellowstones and Yosemites instead of sailing off to continents that are alien property, or to minute and barren islands not worth entering on the map.

There is ground for complaint, as a survey of the indexes of scholarly periodicals reveals quickly. None of our previous conclusions are affected, for we have been careful from the beginning to insist that the critic use his bullion or copper coin in the home market. The article on Wordsworth as a business man was noticed only as an example of what is not our subject. Nevertheless, we shall be helped by a recapitulation of charges brought against "outer" study to understand the motives of "inner" critics and to recognize the assumptions underlying many of their analyses.

J. E. Spingarn's fairly representative objection in *The New Criticism* to research in the race, the time, and the environment as causes of literature grew out of a feeling that literature should be studied as art. "To study these phases of a work of art is to treat it as an historic or social document, and the result is a contribution to the history of culture or civilization, without primary interest for

the history of art.["] A similar conviction appears to underlie the books and articles of Cleanth Brooks. "I have
argued," says Mr. Brooks somewhat more tolerantly, in
a recent essay, "that the critic needs the help of the historian—all the help that he can get; but I have insisted
that the poem has to be read as a poem."[2] Or, more technically, in words written by an eminent contemporary
aesthetician with reference primarily to the plastic arts
but capable of extension to literature: the aim of aesthetics is

> intelligent acquaintance with the presented surface
> of the world instead of intelligent understanding and
> control of physical processes. What it does is to show
> the sorts of relations among sensory elements in
> virtue of which structures, sensuous and immediate,
> are apprehended and felt in their concreteness.[3]

The work of literary art (it is argued) should be analyzed
as a structure, with the least possible reliance on external
information.* Its being is what primarily counts, not
its becoming; its being, moreover, as a self-subsistent
and autotelic organism, not as a part of some larger body
of experience which contains it.

The view that the intrinsic nature of literature is critically more significant than its relation to an environment
is by no means confined to America and England. It has
had articulate champions on the continent, especially,
perhaps, among the French, who were the first to explore
la race, le milieu, and *le moment,* and ever since have
continued to produce responsible literary history. Even
when Taine's influence was at its height there were dis-
senting voices. Flaubert remarked that in La Harpe's
time critics were grammarians and in Taine's and Sainte-
Beuve's they were historians; when, he asked, would
they be artists and nothing but artists?[4] Later, when a
strong resistance to historical methods was developing
in the United States and England, Michel Dragomires-

---

* This view begs the question whether literature is only or essentially
art—a question to which we shall recur in chapter 10.

cou, of the University of Bucharest, in a three-volume work, entitled *La Science de la littérature* (French in language and literary backgrounds if not in geographical origin), argued strongly against the propriety of allowing critical attention to shift from aesthetic qualities to the evolution of national or human consciousness.[5] It seemed to him that the primary critical aim, the achievement of aesthetic insights into literature, was not helped by "allusions to contemporary facts, all that dense network which unites the work to what is not itself, all that historical baggage which weights the notes of our learned— above all, our 'scholarly'—editions."[6] Finally, Philippe Van Tieghem,[7] after reviewing the stages of a controversy carried on for three years in the pages of the *Romanic Review*, announced his support of the antihistorical party. "Literary" works, he asserted, "are not signs of anything but themselves . . . and in theory express nothing but themselves." The critic ought not to be like people who go to the theater to observe the audience.

In my opinion, the important thing is to take one's stand in the text, to lie in watch over it, to search for the value of every word, every effect, every phrase. We must discover relationships and disengage the harmony founded on them, make evident a thousand shades of feeling and thought where the common reader sees only a happy expression, disengage a beauty of detail which the author has neglected to emphasize, show the bearing of ideas which he could have deepened or developed without destroying the proportions or violating the laws of type, analyze the multiple elements of a spiritual state which the author has transmitted as a living synthesis.[8]

The movement to criticize literature with the least possible consideration of its social and intellectual environment is, then, international and powerful.[9] The validity of the arguments summarized above cannot be considered at present; it is enough to observe that the partisans of intrinsic analysis are just now strongly entrenched in their positions. In the remainder of the chapter we shall examine the methods of inner study in order to round out and complete, cursorily but in terms which will permit any amount of imaginative expansion, a survey of analytical reference frames.

It must be recalled before we proceed further that no criticism is ever completely inner, since every critic brings prior attitudes and modes of consciousness to his undertaking. An awareness of this fact is shown by some of the theorists whose arguments have been cited, notably by Van Tiegham, who quotes with evident approval some relevant comments by Bernard Faÿ:

> It is in vain to say that you form no hypothesis, for you could not undertake research unless you were guided by a plan, a preconceived idea, an expectation, or the determination to restrict yourself to a certain period—which is itself a judgment and a hypothesis ... One of the greatest weaknesses of scientific literary history appears to me to be its unawareness of the utility of hypotheses and its attempt to do without them.[20]

Yet there is a reasonably clear and manageable distinction between nonhistorical criticism which brings to its task a body of previously organized theory, and nonhistorical criticism which tries, so far as the conditions of thought permit, to obtain fuller understanding of a literary subject by rearranging and interpreting materials found inside it. Thus a doctrinaire aesthetics normally leads to extrinsic study in precisely the same way as a doctrinaire ethics or politics, whereas a willingness to let the guiding hypothesis rise out of the subject matter leads to inner study.

The inner critic has, essentially, only two choices of procedure. First, he may elect to make discoveries about a single aspect of the literature he intends to study. The number of aspects available for separate investigation cannot be estimated, for more become recognizable as critics' eyes become sharpened to perceive them. Or, if he prefers, he may address himself to two or more aspects; and if he does this he will presumably draw the parts of his analysis together by asserting relationships among them. More briefly, he may analyze a single aspect in isolation or split the object into two or more aspects which are made to comment on each other. (He can hardly discuss more than one aspect without making each throw light on the others, or his study will disintegrate, as do many student papers, into unconnected sections.)

The subject matter, thus determined, may be discussed either with or without a considerable reliance on critical intuitions. At one extreme stands such a treatise as William Empson's *Seven Types of Ambiguity*, which admits so much sheer mind stuff, so to speak, that to many readers it seems culpably subjective. At the other extreme are tabulations of run-on lines and feminine endings in Shakespeare's plays, studies of language like Professor Kittredge's *Observations on the Language of Chaucer's Troilus*, and the graphic and statistical investigations described in Edith Rickert's *New Methods for the Study of Literature*.[11] Most intrinsic criticism falls somewhere between the extremes, inclining perhaps toward the subjective. For the past two decades, especially, a curiosity about inner qualities has tended to be accompanied by a real or imagined sensitivity to overtones, with the result that inner study is less likely than outer study to produce unshakable convictions. The certainty that the "Dear Child" addressed in Wordsworth's "beauteous evening" sonnet was the poet's illegitimate daughter Caroline is greater than the certainty that, as an inner critic has said, she was "filled with an unconscious sympathy for *all* of nature, not merely the grandiose and solemn."[12] The importance of the two bits of knowledge (if both are true) to a full, evaluated apprehension of the sonnet is of course quite another question. At any rate, it is worth noting that one cause of the continuing dispute about the "new" criticism, which tends strongly to the use of inner reference frames,[13] is its propensity for dealing in perceptions not communicable to all readers.

Among the inner aspects of literature which may be discussed in isolation may be mentioned, as current favorites, imagery, irony, ambiguity or multivalence, the use of metaphors and symbols, and tensions of various kinds; but form and texture may be focused in innumerable ways, any one of which may serve as the basis of a penetrating (or highly dubious) essay. Habitual readers of criticism will recall studies of theme, of characterization, of plot, of rhythmic patterns, of style, of the handling of time, of the manipulation of a point of view, of thematic variation in the use of ideas, fictive incidents, and symbols, of idiosyncratic techniques (as, for example, sprung rhythm by Gerard Manley Hopkins). Articles on such topics fill the pages of "advanced" journals like the *Kenyon* and *Sewanee* reviews. A methodology common to many of the articles is easy to describe, if not to use. A body of literature—often, but not invariably, a single work or a number of works by a single author—engages the critic's attention; he has an "insight" into it (that is, he observes something in it or formulates an interpretive hypothesis about it); he searches within the object for means of testing the insight or establishing the hypothesis; and, finally, he writes his essay or book, setting his data within a matrix of commentary that may contain much or little of what has been called sheer mind stuff but in theory is intended merely to place the data in sharp relief.

Since the defenses of inner study quoted earlier turned on the right of literature to be criticized as art, I have been speaking as though only aspects of form or texture could be investigated separately. In actual fact, the opportunities are much broader. Attention may very well be engaged by an aspect of content. What is said in Tennyson's *Idyls* about the responsibilities of kingship?

53

Is Pope's *Essay on Criticism* ideologically self-consistent? How is Heaven characterized in *The Pilgrim's Progress*? Questions like these lead almost inevitably to a consideration of the ideas in literature. Again, the critic may interest himself in what is implied, rather than explicitly stated, in a work or series of works. Do Falstaff's actions justify the belief that he is a coward? What view of marriage is suggested by *Pride and Prejudice*? Can an ontology be exhumed from Milton's epics? There is utility in all such studies, if only because, as Bernard Faÿ has said, "Literary works rust and become dull after a certain period of use. They must be revivified, looked at again from a new point of view. . . . They must be illuminated ceaselessly by differing hypotheses which throw them into vivid relief and rejuvenate them in proportion as their vigor becomes exhausted."[14] Almost any new interest can refresh our sense of a familiar work and, by opening our eyes to an aspect of the work's totality which has hitherto escaped notice or been conceived of in a traditional way, deepen intellectual and emotional apprehension.

If, instead of remaining intent on one aspect only, the inner critic compares two or more, his procedure may be the same except that he goes through it more than once and discovers relationships inhering among the separate bodies of findings. Thus a poem's imagery may be found to clarify or confuse its theme, a novel's plot to pull against or reinforce an implied world view, a play's tempo to be appropriate or inappropriate to a mood suggested by the dialogue. Undergraduate students of literature use a parody of this second method when, in criticizing an assigned poem, they discuss in successive paragraphs subject, metrical form, imagery, irony, rhythmic effects, and tone (or whatever other topics they have been led by class discussions to believe important). The professional critic rarely addresses himself to so many aspects in a single piece of critical writing; he is vividly aware of the values of self-limitation, and by foreseeing an end from the beginning avoids the necessity of listing a series of unresolved conclusions in his final paragraph. Nevertheless, there is often a fundamental similarity between his method and that of the student. The chief practical differences are that the professional critic's perceptions are keener, his attention is less scattered, and all his findings are at last pulled together. His conclusion may be an evaluation, but if so the evaluation is derived from a total analytic finding, as, for example, that a work is tightly unified or contradicts in one aspect what it asserts in another.

Only one kind of internal reference frame requires further comment. The word "intention" is used by critics in two senses, one of which has relevance to intrinsic study whereas the other has not.

If a literary intention is established by study of an author's notebooks, correspondence, or critical commentary of any kind on his own work, the reference frame is obviously external, not internal, and the critique for which it provides an expository framework will be of the type described in the preceding chapter. A number of recent critics mean by "intention," however, not a conscious aim present in the author's mind during the act of composition but something implicit in the work itself—very much what other critics mean when they speak of "subject." An intention of this latter kind is not imposed upon the work but discovered in it; and criticism resulting from an analysis centering upon implicit purpose is therefore in the strictest sense internal.

The distinction between an author's intention and that of his work has been remarked on by several of the comparatively few critics who have discussed critical methodologies in the abstract. Thus Richard Moulton: "The conscious purpose of a poet—if he has one—belongs to his biography; what criticism means by 'purpose' and 'design' is the purpose particular parts are seen to serve in the poetic product when analyzed."[15] J. E. Spingarn makes essentially the same point.

55

The poet's real "intention" is to be found, not in one or another of the various ambitions that flit through his mind, but in the actual work of art which he creates. His poem is his "intention." In any other sense, "intention" is outside the aesthetic field—a mere matter of the poet's literary theory or his power of will.[16]

Louis Cazamian, who wished the critic to concern himself with the *idée génératrice* of individual works, nevertheless recognized that the idea may have been partly unconscious:

> Criticism mainly consists in realizing, through the power of attention, a complex of intellectual adaptations and sequences which had remained largely obscure in the mind that had lived them first. Hence that paradoxical, but by no means infrequent occurrence: the critic better aware than the author of the purpose and trend of a book.[17]

Finally, in the opinion of a mechanistic aesthetician, "a motive has a degree of determinateness and in the end is properly named not by the imagined goal which its ignorance may identify as its intention, but by what it comes to accomplish."[18] The "intentional fallacy"[19] is accordingly not committed by all critics who make much of intention, but only by those who locate purpose outside the aesthetic object, in the often erring intelligence of the creative artist.

Implicit intention provides an internal reference frame of great usefulness, since the attempt to analyze what D. W. Prall has called "the unitary effect that is the actual character of [the] aesthetic object"[20] prevents the shifting of the critical focus from the ostensible literary subject to something related but tangential. There is a value in this, for, as Philippe Van Tieghem, whose short volume is full of acute observations, has pointed out, the study of literature eventuates all too often in knowledge which really illuminates something quite different from the object that provoked the original interest.

> It comes about, astonishingly, that one finds it
> more agreeable and truly instructive to speak of
> Stendhal or Dante with a cultivated and reflective
> man of taste . . . than with a specialist who has done
> much research on Stendhal, or one who is remark-
> ably well informed about the political affairs of the
> Whites and the Blacks.[21]

The referring of all the analytic findings to a single controlling concept supplied by the creative work itself
effectively answers this protest. In the best intentional
criticism there is a largeness, a sweep, that is conspicu-
ously lacking from attempts to illuminate only fractional
aspects. This is the approach urged by such aestheticians
as Bosanquet and Samuel Alexander, and practiced with
great skill by Percy Lubbock in *The Craft of Fiction,* a
work to which I have already alluded as one of the critical classics of our century.

The amount of literature which the inner critic under-
takes to analyze in one of the ways described may range
from a single brief work to a great many long ones.
Robert Wooster Stallman's article, "Hardy's Hour-Glass
Novel,"[22] likens the plot of a specific novel to a geometric
figure; E. M. Forster's chapter on plot in *Aspects of the
Novel*[23] discusses plot generally, as one element in most
fiction. William Empson's analysis of Marvell's short
poem, "The Garden,"[24] runs to nearly the length of R. P.
Warren's essay, "Pure and Impure Poetry," which seems
to bear on all poetry.[25] Thus it cannot be said that inner
criticism consistently, or even characteristically, differs
from outer criticism in proposing to get to the bottom of
individual works. Large quantities of inner criticism attempt to illuminate conventions, genres, rhetorical techniques, and the like, conceived in terms of more than one
work or even in terms of all literature.

It may be added finally that the use of internal reference frames by large numbers of practicing critics has
begun comparatively recently. In part the development
is an outgrowth of post-Kantian aesthetics; in part it is

related to what A. O. Lovejoy has called "diversitarianism" (itself no doubt related to post-Kantian aesthetics)—an interest in the unique characteristics of objects rather than in their conformity to external norms. Behind both influences probably lies the Baconian principle of inductive investigation, which has thrown doubt on the propriety of analysis by reference to *a priori* conceptual frames. At any rate, the methodological trend is presently vigorous.

7

The Choice among Analytic Reference Frames

UP TO THIS POINT it has been seen that analysis can proceed by the use of external or internal reference frames, either singly or in combination—for a complex purpose may require the gathering of more than one kind of data. Without the use of some reference frame, however, there can be no analysis and consequently no rational understanding. The dominant sensory quality of a smile or a look of pain, a fire or a snowplow, can perhaps be absorbed intuitively as a thing-in-itself. One sensory gulp and the cognitive act is over. Rational knowledge, on the contrary, is dependent on an awareness of relationships, and relationships can be apprehended only by the adjustment of details to one another, either within a whole or within aspects of two or more wholes.

So far we can proceed confidently. But when we inquire what kinds of reference frames are most productive of rational understanding, we are confronted by serious problems. Which of all the conceivable varieties of understanding do we most want? Since complete apprehension of even a single literary work is impossible, we must choose, must adapt our analytic means to an end; and ends are determined by desires, among which it is hard to arbitrate on purely logical grounds.

An example will set the difficulty in relief. If, by the use of an internal reference frame, I illuminate brilliantly the aesthetic structure of Pope's *Rape of the Lock*, I will seem, to a person especially drawn (shall we say) to the history of ideas, to have neglected everything of greatest importance in the work. Conversely, if by using external reference frames I show that the poem makes popular eighteenth-century assumptions about art, society, and the nature and duties of man, I will seem, to a person whose chief literary interest is formal, to have skirted the central problem. Nothing is commoner than to hear conflicting opinions about the usefulness of analytic findings. "Magnificent!" pronounces one judge of a critical book or article. "Opens new vistas!" "Really?" asks another, with humorously elevated eyebrows. "I thought it rather trivial." From the standpoint of his own interest, each is probably right; and each could justify his interest by a long process of reasoning which was perfectly self-consistent but rested ultimately on a nonrational preference—the value atmosphere of a boyhood home, possibly, or the instinctive cravings of a physiological organism (for repose, for stimulus, for a sharper focus of energy, and so on).

The search for a principle of choice among competing interests, by requiring an act of evaluation, accordingly leads directly into the realm of values. We are forbidden, however, to enter that realm by the earlier decision to separate the theory of analysis from that of evaluation. Thus we find ourselves in a dilemma from which we can extricate ourselves only in two ways, neither entirely satisfactory.

First, it is possible to dodge the problem actually central to the chapter and put readers off with an invitation to choose as they see fit among the reference frames already discussed, taking care to make the selections which will best serve their primary interests. We might say, for example, that an interest in form leads usually to the study of stresses, tensions, balances, resolutions, and the like and therefore suggests—indeed, almost requires—an examination of inward-pointing meanings, whereas an interest in literature as a source of ideas motivates a checking of the ideas by application to extra-literary situations or propositions. An attempt might be made to classify all the conceivable varieties of analytic interest and to comment knowingly on the best ways of exploiting each. Again, still within the limits of the first alternative, a series of advisory statements might be made about a theoretically "best" method of approach to the exploitation of every interest. The critic ought to ascertain whether his text is the best obtainable, to satisfy himself that its attribution to an author is correct, to obtain an adequate understanding of the time and circumstances of composition, to compile a bibliography of critical and historical writings on the subject, and so on. By following either plan it would be easy to fill a dozen pages with suggestions for practical action. I fear, however, that the suggestions would neither very much enlighten the reader nor stimulate him to rethink his assumptions in such a manner as to broaden or deepen his criticism.

It will be better, I think, to take the alternative way out and assert an evaluative criterion for the judgment of reference frames, even though in doing so we violate in some degree the theoretical distinctness of our basic categories. The decision is the less disturbing because a criterion is implied by the definition given earlier of the ideal critical goal. If the goal of analysis is complete apprehension of the literary subject matter, the better analytic methods are necessarily those which lead to quantitatively greater understanding. Now it is undoubtedly true that from one point of view the greatness or smallness of a body of critical knowledge can be estimated only by reference to the capacity of the knowledge to satisfy a specific interest, just as a quantity of bricks may be thought large or small depending on whether the bricks are to be used for building a fireplace or a house. From another point of view, however, sizes can be measured against each other without regard to anything except themselves. A truckload of boards is larger, in an understandable sense, than a potful of coffee, a street larger than a bench, a bookcase larger than an ashtray. In exactly the same way, an explication of Shakespeare's moral universe is critically larger—that is to say, it leads to greater quantities of analytic knowledge—than a discovery about the Italian background of *The Merry Wives of Windsor*. The example is extreme, and an attempt to establish the comparative size of half a dozen critical conclusions would probably lead to fruitless argument. Nevertheless, the concept of critical size is not meaningless. It can be talked about, if not very concretely, at least in general terms. We must talk about it here; for the only standard accessible for the judgment of reference frames without a long detour through value theory is the quantitative standard implicit in our definition of the ideal critical goal. What we want is the fullest possible apprehension, the greatest possible illumination. Reference frame *A* is superior to reference frame *B* if it results in greater amounts of understanding, inferior if it results in less.

The principle is no sooner stated than a perplexity arises. The larger critical conclusions are often more controversial than the smaller ones: the discovery about the Italian background of *The Merry Wives* may be ir-refutably "true," the explication of Shakespeare's moral universe unconvincing. We ought, therefore, to take into consideration the difference between positive and doubtful knowledge; otherwise we will be forced into preferring the wildest general hypothesis to the most painstaking study of particulars. If a particular may turn out to be permanently useful and a general hypothesis to be useless or worse than useless, it would be a mistake to prefer all hypotheses to all studies of particulars on the ground that the former would be more illuminating if correct.

One may infer from their practice that for the last three generations or so large numbers of academic critics have believed all generalizations to be potentially wild. Within the larger universities, at least, there has been a feeling that criticism ought to start where the physical sciences had started earlier and accumulate inductively, bit by painful bit, masses of unquestionable particulars. There may have been faith that eventually, when immense quantities of data were in, generalizations could again be risked; but in the meantime a critical discovery was to be judged "good" if it admitted no doubt, "bad" if contradictory evidence could be found. The best way of advancing toward the ultimate goal seemed to be not by igniting huge bonfires near the head of the trail but by setting out a series of little torches which could be relied on to shed tiny circles of brightness along the way. In the end one would get farthest so, in the humane disciplines as in the physical sciences; there would be no serious accidents, and progress, although gradual, would be sure. Accordingly, serious scholars (who were critics whenever their researches illuminated literary texts and not merely literary backgrounds) turned away from general interests to the study of details, usually in terms of a historical context.

Such appears to have been the theory, and I suppose there will be agreement both that it provided a plausible working hypothesis for students of literature and that the men and women who submitted themselves to it exercised a noble restraint over their natural impatience. Neither can it be denied that the disciplines have led to notable triumphs, especially in interpreting our older literature. Chaucer's explicit meanings are now mostly within the comprehension of anyone willing to read Professor Robinson's notes; Shakespeare's plays have been clarified by studies of Elizabethan idiom and contemporary stage techniques; Spenser's *Faerie Queene* has been put into a rich context of contemporary rhetoric and historical incidents; Milton's poetry has been irradiated by biographical, theological, political, and rhetorical studies. And yet everyone who is acquainted with the present critical situation is aware that in the last dozen or fifteen years there has been a general rush to light bonfires. There has been, indeed, a widespread disillusionment with "scientific" methods, at least among young scholars, with the result that in many departments of English an uncomfortable tension has developed between the lighters of torches and the igniters of bonfires.

The movement seems to have been stimulated by a conviction that the torches set out by older critics have all too often been placed along tracks that lead endlessly across plains instead of upward toward summits. What purposes besides those of "getting something published" and winning academic advancement have been served (the younger critics seem by their actions to inquire) by the typical discovery of a partial source, a trivial influence, a conceivable allusion on the third or fourth plane of meaning? It is not hard to understand a feeling that the accumulation of such discoveries in the tens or hundreds of thousands would hardly advance us at all toward answering any of the deeper questions that might be asked about literature. Surely no one except a born antiquarian ever embarked on the serious study of literature in the hope of obtaining information of the kind many scholarly journals seem especially eager to supply—information, for example, about the relation of the Wife of Bath's opinions on marriage to those expressed in Jerome's treatise *Adversus Jovinianum,* or a possible model for Shakespeare's Shallow. It is as though the student of architecture were encouraged to spend his time identifying the origin of the stones put together in striking architectural forms, or the student of painting to analyze the construction of Rembrandt's easel. If the facts obtainable through such inquiries satisfied any vital interest, the tedium of the critical processes necessary to arrive at them would be accepted with reasonable grace. Unfortunately they often do not. The suspicion is unavoidable that large numbers of "experts" have given up the attempt to find answers to questions that anybody actually wishes to ask, and instead have sought industriously for questions to fit the answers their methods allow them to supply. But this is to reverse the proper relationship of methods and interests. The methods ought clearly to be adapted to interests, not the interests to be subordinated to methods. To praise a method regardless of the problem (says Kenneth Burke) is like advocating the use of nothing but quadratic equations.[1]

The protests against external study cited in the preceding chapter clearly imply dissatisfaction with an unfruitful devotion to "scientific" methods; but the objection has often been made explicit. Thus Louis Cazamian asserted that philological and historical approaches "are not the divinely-appointed rulers to the whole empire of criticism."[2] Michel Dragomirescou believed the historical method to become "absolutely destructive when applied to the study of masterpieces."[3] W. C. Brownell thought the detective method "debased."[4] The contempt of some of the "new" critics for historical drudgery is notorious. Yet there are serious difficulties in the way of lighting bonfires, much as one may be inclined to agree that the illumination from torches often does not fall on paths that lead to a view.

One difficulty is in learning where materials suitable for bonfires are to be gathered and how the match is to be applied. Granted that literature is not in its deepest nature either history or philology, what is it, and how can the critic best come to grips with it? To this question I shall offer one possible answer in a moment. Another, and at first glance perhaps even more puzzling, difficulty is that in proportion as one exploits larger interests one moves away from certainty toward the area of merely probable conjecture. The implications of this second problem may be considered immediately.

The reason why trivial problems are easier to solve "truthfully" than large ones is that the trivial is less inextricably involved, by reason of its small size and lack of importance, with things not itself. It can be isolated more successfully than the significant because, like an inert gas, it does not enter into combinations in which it partly loses its identity. Its existence makes little real difference to the whole of which it is a part. The significant (with which in the present discussion we may identify the large) stands, however, at the head of a long train of successive consequences or infuses that with which it coexists. The attempt to discover the first of a series of causes requires not one act of analysis but many, therefore opens many opportunities for error; and the infused is harder to isolate for separate discussion than the merely included, as a solution can be resolved into its parts less easily than a walnut can be picked out of a salad. Accordingly, if the smaller discoveries tend toward "truth," the larger discoveries tend always toward hypothesis.

In the physical sciences the usefulness of hypotheses has long been recognized. Newton's theory of gravity, Darwin's theory of evolution, and Einstein's theory of relativity have all been working assumptions rather than established facts. The first two, indeed, were seen in time to require considerable revision, as the third in its turn very well may. Yet for a number of years each provided a coherent framework for enormous quantities of verifiable data and at the same time indicated a direction for further research. These are obvious examples; but even small items of scientific knowledge often contain an element of hypothesis. In experience it is not true that light and heavy objects fall at equal speeds, or that pulleys and screws work without friction, or that water contains nothing but oxygen and hydrogen. The situations that occur in everyday life are regularly simplified in order to be made comprehensible. There is even mythology in inductive science. The virus which is held responsible for the common cold and other diseases was for a long time pure hypothesis, differing from earlier fictions about illness chiefly in positing the existence of submicroscopic organisms that work chemically instead of spiritual entities that work by volition. And what is true of scientific thought is true of other kinds of thought that aspire to scientific certainty. Classical economics made the sacrifice of pretending that human beings were mere coveting machines—a principle so transparently untrue to the facts of daily experience that Ruskin thought the knowledge in which it eventuated worthless.[5] Psychology is hagridden by hypotheses, many of which, to do them justice, have been fruitful. No area of thought is completely objective. The American belief in democracy originated quite as much in philosophical speculation about government as in the observation of specific political scenes. Few general ideas prove minutely and permanently "true"; but before being superseded many have reduced enormously the sum total of human ignorance.

If, then, the difficulty of making large discoveries has been met in all departments of extraliterary thought by the development in the best minds of a receptive attitude toward promising hypotheses, why should not critics cultivate a similar attitude? Every analytic generalization about literature—individual works, the total literary output of individual writers, movements, conventions, techniques, and possibly even literature as a special kind of human activity—must remain subject to review in the light of known facts; and no doubt many or most will eventually be found wanting. There ought not to be, however, as at present there indisputably is, a tendency in authoritative quarters to reject the very idea of hypotheses with indignation or contempt. If criticism is to be generically rather than exceptionally a significant human activity instead of an ivory-tower occupation of professional antiquarians, it must tolerate movements in the direction of meaningful synthesis. It cannot rest permanently at the stage reached by certain physical sciences in the early eighteenth century, when virtuosi collected shells, rocks, fossils, and insects more or less at hazard, presumably on the assumption that someone might eventually find a use for their discoveries. Critical articles which remove small opacities or correct small misunderstandings of course deserve a continuing place in our academic critical journals. The greater usefulness of analytic processes which illuminate large aspects of wholes instead of outlying parts is clearly implicit, however, in the recognition that the better analytic reference frames are those which lead to greater quantities of critical understanding.

We return now to the former of the two difficulties, that of knowing which of the nonhistorical and non-philological aspects of literature has a special claim to attention and what method of approach to it is most feasible. There is no need to insist on a wholly new kind of interest, since the foregoing reflections have led merely to the conclusion that skepticism about hypothetical knowledge ought not to inspire an exclusive concentration on details. Nevertheless, I believe that an important aspect of literature has seldom been given the critical attention it deserves, and I propose, therefore, in the remaining paragraphs of the present chapter, to recommend briefly to notice an internal reference frame which will permit it to be exploited—how successfully depends both on the creative work chosen for discussion and on the critic's ability to perceive sensitively and explain lucidly.

A method of approach can be found through a widely accepted view (to be recurred to later in another context) that art is a way of knowing. We learn about the universe of experience through our perceptions quite as much as through the exercise of discursive reason. The greater part of our knowledge may in fact be perceptual; we learn about people, clothes, houses, cities, climates, and many other aspects of our total environment principally through the senses. The devaluing of immediate perceptions, to which the whole modern educational process strongly tends, is a great misfortune, since it results in the partial closing of one of our two main windows on the universe. "Truth" consists of more than a series of logical propositions or the objective physical phenomena to which they refer. It includes also the feel of specific situations and the sensory qualities of the situations which provoke the feeling responses. We could become more richly aware of our universe, more vibrantly alive in it, and perhaps better able to control both it and ourselves if we increased our sensitivity to percepts. For this reason it has sometimes been suggested, as by Herbert Read in *The Grassroots of Art*,⁶ that our educational system should be basically aesthetic and not basically ratiocinative.

Literature is more than an art, and it would be absurd to argue that in criticizing all literary texts primary stress should be placed on the interpretation of sensory data. The prose of Milton, Burke, and Ruskin, for example, is fundamentally ratiocinative, though much of it belongs to the literature of power rather than to the literature of knowledge. The typical imaginative or "creative" work, in contrast, makes most of its statements about experience not by logical propositions but by presenting the experience itself so that the reader can sense its meanings directly as percepts. The difference between art and nonart might, indeed, be located precisely here: a literary work is art so far as its meanings are presented as percepts; nonart (the word is not to be taken as depreciatory) so far as its meanings are defined in ratiocinative terms. But the vast majority of readers, including perhaps most teachers and critics (and certainly myself), are by no means really at home with percepts. Their cognitive processes have been so unevenly developed, their sensory mechanisms so disregarded and even deprecated through years of rational schooling, that perceptual data acquire clear meaning for them only when translated into logical propositions.

One highly important function of criticism, accordingly, is that of mediating between art and a reading public largely incapable of recognizing aesthetic meanings or accepting anything but ratiocinative assertions as knowledge. Although this is not the only function, or even the only important function, its usefulness seems to me especially great at a time when most conservative criticism is historical and much "advanced" criticism psychoanalytic or rather mechanically formal. What, for instance, is the essential meaning of *King Lear*? University students who are absorbed by the play on a first reading often sense obscurely that it says something important about life; but when they come to class hoping to learn more clearly what the something is, they are usually put off with answers to other questions in which they feel little or no interest. They are told that the play was entered in the Stationers' Register on November 26, 1607; that the ultimate source is Geoffrey of Monmouth's *Historia Regum Britanniae;* that Gloucester was borrowed from Sidney's *Arcadia;* that Lamb thought the play unactable; that Lear's insanity is very carefully prepared for; that his tragic fault is rashness; that the subplot is closely related to the main plot; that the climax comes in the storm scene; that Edgar's disguise is in accord with a contemporary convention; that "fool," in the King's last speech, has been taken by most commentators to refer to Cordelia; and so on. Much of this information is potentially useful, even indispensable; but too often it simply provides the instructor with a way of filling up the class hours without thinking about the essential meaning of the dramatic situations individually and of the play as a whole. Yet it is the powerfully expressed meanings that make the play really profound, really vital. If readers could be helped, by a criticism which separated the various strands of the action and interpreted each individually and then all in formal combination, not only to see more deeply into the source of the play's power but also to acquire the ability in life to learn through perceptions as well as through the reason, the critical exposition would itself have the richest possible human significance.

I suggest, then, that the critic who is not already committed to another interest look in this direction for his analytical method of dealing with imaginative works that seem to pose no special problems. The interpretation of the complex total perception to which the reading of a novel or play may lead can make accessible to the intelligence, and therefore rationally communicable, knowledge that otherwise would remain confined to parts of the consciousness able to express themselves only by ambiguous ejaculations. On a small scale, everybody is familiar with the usefulness of such interpretations. We may describe the sight of a livid face by saying, "Frank became very angry," or the slamming about of toys in an upstairs bedroom by remarking, "Winifred could hardly stand being kept home from kindergarten because of her cold." On the much larger scale required in critical discussion of a literary work which evokes not one isolated perception but hundreds or thousands in interrelation, the analytic process is much more difficult. Nevertheless, rational interpretations of imaginative literary works can be made, and they satisfy, better than analysis of any other sort, the quantitative criterion for the judgment of reference frames. No knowledge of a work can be greater than an understanding of what, in all its parts and as a totality, it *means*. The method avoids, furthermore, as well as any nonhistorical and nonphilological critical process can, the temptation to abandon observation for pure speculation. I do not, certainly, think abstract speculation frivolous, or I should not have undertaken the writing of this book. I recognize, however, and honor, the yearning of many minds for concretions; and it is in concretions that the conclusions accessible through the variety of internal analysis just described must be anchored.

8

Moving from Analysis to Evaluation

So FAR we have been concerned with the theory of critical analysis. Criticism was defined, however, as having for its ultimate goal a full, evaluated apprehension of its subject matter. We cannot, therefore, rest satisfied with a study of analytic methods, but must move on to a consideration of the theory of value. In terms of the visual metaphor used in chapter 4, we must shift our attention from critical assertions which are sustained from below to those which are suspended from above. There will be difficulties, for the cables are less easily visible than the columns. The very persons who have hung objects from the cables seem often to be unaware of their existence and may sometime be seen pointing with satisfaction to shadows which they mistake for pillars. We must peer very intently into the half-darkness in the hope of discerning the actualities of the supports. Our aim will be to find a common ground of some kind for both pillars and cables—some means of passing logically from description to appraisal, from analytic findings about literature to evaluative interpretation of the data.

It is important at the outset to make clear exactly what is to be understood by "evaluation." In conversation, and perhaps in formal writing also, the word is often applied to remarks that seem in any way to hint judgments. If I say, for example, that a novel is conventional, I may be thought to have implied disapproval. If I go further and assert roundly, "The characters are wooden, the actions frequently unmotivated, the ending contrived, the tone frigid, the style involved, and the total effect confusing," I will certainly be thought to have censured, perhaps even to have denounced. Nevertheless, the difficulties in the way of making such statements are those of analysis, not of evaluation. Each of the descriptive terms can be made responsible to a readily acceptable definition, and the appropriateness of its use in the context can be established by investigation. Thus, for example, "wooden" can be defined to mean "visibly responsive to an external will; without apparent power of self-direction." The problem of determining whether in this sense the characters in the novel are wooden can be solved without reference to the reader's value sense. If the inquiry is delicate, it is not so delicate that patient and sensitive exertion by one or more critics is incapable of carrying it to a successful conclusion. And so with all the other items in the description. By connoting instead of denoting a judgment I have thrown the burden of evaluating on the reader, whom I may expect, but do not require, to believe that valuable novels cannot be like this one. Even the last item in the statement, that the novel's total effect is confusing, permits the discovery of objective correlatives of the descriptive term without recourse to a value sense. Confusion is not only a state of mind but also a condition of things. In a novel, confusion may result from disorder, or from ambiguity (the novelist seems not to know what to make of the situations he has himself imagined), or from self-contradiction (he implies opposite meanings, outcomes, or attitudes, and never succeeds in resolving his uncertainty). Every one of the terms—"wooden," "unmotivated," "contrived," "frigid," "involved," "confused"—is thus basically analytic, not basically evaluative, and has relevance to the part of the critical process already discussed, not to the part we are about to consider.

The logical status of such critical adjectives as "interesting," "charming," "delightful," "repulsive," "deplorable," "displeasing," and, supereminently, "good" and "bad," "valuable" and "valueless," is quite different. None of these terms can be tied to an objective correlative without danger of arousing immediate and irresolvable controversy. The correlative of each is subjective. A book is interesting if it interests—but what properties must it have to interest? A reply to the question must be sought less in the book than in the reader. "Confuse" is defined in its first sense in a reputable college dictionary[1] as "to combine without order or clearness; jumble; render indistinct." If the materials of a novel are combined without order or clearness, if they are jumbled or rendered indistinct, the book may properly be called confusing; and whether they are so combined, jumbled, or made indistinct, can be decided by analysis. "Interest," however, is defined in the same dictionary (which is representative of all) as "to engage or excite the attention or curiosity of: *a story which interested him greatly.* To concern (a person, etc.) in something; involve," etc. The primary reference here is not to a perceived object but to a perceiving human subject. And so with "charming," "delightful," "repulsive," "deplorable," "displeasing," and a host of similar adjectives used in critical writing. All these terms describe human attitudes—attitudes, clearly, with value implications—rather than objective properties discoverable in literary documents. So too with "good" and "bad," "valuable" and "valueless." It is true that one large aim of value studies is to determine the objective characteristics of the good and the valuable, the bad and the valueless, so as to make possible a confident discrimination between the good and the nongood. The aim, however, has not yet become an accomplishment, at least so far as literature is concerned. In ordinary critical parlance the announcement that a book is good may have one or more of an almost infinite variety of meanings: "I like it"; "Though it doesn't appeal to me, I approve of it"; "It's interesting"; "It's thought-provoking"; "It's admirably organized"; "It has an agreeable style"; "It has a strong anti-Communist bias"; "It has a terrific love scene"; "It has had a wide sale"; and so on indefinitely. "Valuable" has a similar though perhaps somewhat narrower range of connotation. While waiting

74

for the achievement of a consensus about the objective correlatives of literary goodness or value, we must, therefore, regard "good" and "bad," "valuable" and "valueless," as belonging with words that denote value attitudes and not with words that describe objective properties. The logical status of such terms will be examined in the remaining chapters.

The difference between evaluation (the statement of value attitudes) and meaningful analysis (the setting in relief of data relevant to the formation of value attitudes) appears evident as soon as stated. Yet it is not certain that the distinction has been generally perceived either by literary critics or by value theorists; and beyond question its importance to critical theory has never been adequately recognized. The word "evaluation" may, of course, be defined in such a way as to include assertions like the one about the "wooden" novel; but in that event only *some* evaluations are subject to the logical difficulties presently to be considered. The part of the total critical process affected by recent studies in the theory of value is accordingly much smaller than might at first be thought. It is the rare critic, however, who never makes direct pronouncements about either total value (the book is "good" or "has value") or partial value (it is "interesting" or "charming" or "delightful"). Conclusions about the logic and techniques of evaluation will therefore have relevance to much criticism and not only to criticism which sets out frankly to assess value.

The naïve view of the relationship between descriptive findings and value judgments is that the former lead directly to the latter. A changed apprehension is thought to result automatically in a changed valuation. This view has a strong foundation both in everyday experience and in philosophical theory. Certain pragmatists have argued that the sense of value may precede analysis and guide the attention in its exploration of the object. My judgment of a friend's necktie is likely to be spontaneous and unreflective and not to be withheld until I have made a study of the tie's design. My judgment of a room which I have just entered for the first time will almost certainly not wait upon a detailed inspection of the furnishings. "How delightful!" I may remark to myself, or "How drab and uninteresting!" Human faces, again, are usually remembered not as distinct shapes but as hard, sympathetic, shrewd, lively, intelligent, and the like, each quality carrying some suggestion for approval or disapproval. Rudolf Arnheim had such experiences in mind when he urged that so-called secondary responses (recognition of violence and passion in a fire) are really primary; what we immediately see in the fire is not a play of color and shape but a "lively, graceful aggressiveness."[2] It is therefore understandable that a psychological critic like I. A. Richards, whose interest is in human responses rather than in critical theory, should believe that evaluation "nearly always settles itself; or rather, our own inmost nature and the nature of the world in which we live decide it for us. Our prime endeavour must be to get the relevant mental condition and see what happens."[3] From this point of view the relation of descriptive data to evaluation presents no problem. We need only be aware that new knowledge and an altered sense of value accompany each other in experience.

Although many immediate value responses have undoubtedly been prepared for by earlier value experiences,[4] these are cogent observations, and I have no wish to dispute them. Nevertheless, they fail actually to touch the present study, which has to do not with the psychology but with the logic of criticism and therefore must give logical priority preference over *de facto*. Our hope is not to discover the psychological mechanisms which touch off critical pronouncements but to gain insight into the rational processes upon which the speculative soundness (if one prefers, the "science") of criticism depends. The critic's commitment, I take it, is to reasonable modes of thought. If he communicates his findings about literature in nonrational ways his writing will be not critical but creative. His essay or book will then be a secondary art work stimulated by a primary one (or more than one), subject to rational analysis and evaluation in the same way as a prose poem or familiar essay, and hence a proper object for the attention of the critic but not for that of the critical theorist. An investigation of the rationale of criticism requires the limitation of the inquiry to discourse which is professedly reasonable; otherwise we are half-beaten from the beginning.

It follows, then, that we cannot avoid confronting honestly the logical relationship of analysis to evaluation, no matter how abstract the considerations into which we are led. Fortunately, for more than half a century value has been subjected to searching philosophical analysis. As early as 1897 Christian von Ehrenfels was able to say that since the time of the ancient Greek and Roman ethical philosophers values had never been so intensively studied.[5] From then until now studies of value have multiplied so rapidly that the student of the subject must plow through a discouraging amount of reading before he feels capable of forming any opinions. Nevertheless, for the most part literary critics have continued blandly to identify literary value with conformity to various classes of expectations without seeming to realize how seriously their basic assumptions have been questioned.

Value theory has to do with such problems as the basic nature of value (is it qualitative or relational? objective or subjective?), the psychic states with which valuing is primarily associated (prizing, interest, liking, satisfaction, pleasure, fulfillment, desire?), the verifiability or unverifiability of value predications (are evaluations logical propositions or emotive ejaculations?), and the motives and dialectics of valuing—in short, with values and the processes of valuing in all their aspects and mutual relations. Modern interest in the problems has arisen (thinks one student) in the hope of overcoming "the dualism between scientific description and human appreciation, partly at least by making the former of service to the

77

latter, in describing and systematizing the various phases of our active and emotional life."[6] The subject's importance (according to another student) is that of "the fuller apprehension, or appreciation, of the significance of anything for everything else"[7]—problem enough, surely, to justify the expenditure of a great deal of intellectual energy. Progress toward a solution of the fundamental cruxes has been in some respects exasperatingly slow. Indeed, a recent symposium, set off by an article which expressed extreme dissatisfaction with the state of value studies, indicates that there is still far more disagreement than agreement.[8] The issues have, however, been clarified, opposing points of view have won articulate champions, and, luckily for our purpose, one set of tentative conclusions has the most direct possible relevance to literary criticism.

The conclusions were stated by Abraham Kaplan in an article published recently in the *Journal of Aesthetics and Art Criticism*.[9] It has become evident as the result of a controversy that there are three prominent theories of the logical relationship between analytic data and evaluative judgments. The relationship has been conceived of as that of logical consequence, as that of verification, and as that of causality. Each of the three theories must detain us briefly.

The theory of logical consequence asserts that evaluation follows by entailment upon the discovery in the art object of qualities previously defined as valuable. If, for example, it has been decided in advance that literature is praiseworthy when it skillfully imitates a recurrent life experience, analysis which shows that a given novel satisfies the criterion entails a favorable critical verdict. In Kaplan's words,

> Among the facts described are some which are the defined equivalents of the appraised value character. The aesthetic value of the object *consists* in its possession of certain properties, so that the statement that it has those properties entails that it is

78

aesthetically valuable. The premise cannot be affirmed and the conclusion denied without contradiction.[10]

The same principle holds equally if the value in question is nonaesthetic.

According to this view, the logical relationship of analysis and appraisal is satisfyingly tight. The difficulty arises in connection with the controlling definition of value. Is it true that literary works deserve approbation whenever they skillfully imitate a recurrent life experience? The mimesis-of-universals aesthetics, however intelligent still, no longer has commanding authority; objections to it will start up at once in many minds. But *no* definition of literary value is now established beyond cavil. At most, there is agreement on a few elementary principles, such as the aesthetic requirement of unity. Unity, however, although very probably a condition of aesthetic value, need not itself constitute the value; moreover, are there not, conceivably, other values which take precedence over the aesthetic? I suppose no one would deny that Henry James's *The Ambassadors* is more tightly unified than Tolstoy's *War and Peace*. Is there agreement that in consequence it is the greater novel?

The longer one reflects on the problem of finding a generally acceptable definition of literary value the more one becomes convinced that David Daiches, in his *New Literary Values*, was right in saying that no such definition exists. No doubt there are definitions that will receive the approval of critical cliques; and some definition is presumably "right" with relation to every complex of nonliterary convictions and attitudes. But it is clear that in the present climate of opinion any evaluation entailed by a dogmatic definition of literary value will lack scientific validity. It will arouse opposition. If our hope is to find an evaluative method which will permit assurance that the appraisal is entailed by analytic data alone, without recourse to dogmatic assertion, the first of the three lines of analysis will not serve us. In Kaplan's words, attempts to justify [definitions of value] as *analyses* of the properties are, as G. E. Moore has shown in the case of ethical values, doomed to failure. For it *is* in fact possible to affirm the descriptive premise and deny the appraisive conclusion. Whether or not this is self-contradictory is precisely the point at issue, and the question cannot be begged."[11]

The second theory is that of verification; the data discovered in analysis constitute evidence for an appraisal. "Every appraisal is a hypothesis, and the descriptive materials confirm or disconfirm it. The description does not entail the appraisal, but gives it more or less evidential weight."[12] Let us follow the implications of this theory in two evaluative hypotheses of qualitatively different types.

We will begin by imagining the hypothesis to be that such-and-such a novel is "interesting"—for I trust it will be conceded that the awakening of interest is a value. I undertake, then, to justify the hypothesis by finding corroborative evidence. How am I to recognize such evidence when I see it?

The usual way is to assume that the quality "interest" is an invariable concomitant of a certain type of subject matter or a certain method of treatment—for example, romantic intrigue, or a skillful building up of suspense. Two objections to this procedure suggest themselves. First, there may be disagreement about the assumption. Some readers are bored, not interested, by romantic intrigue. Not everyone appreciates narrative skill; those who do not will lack interest in fiction which for many pages withholds the resolution of complications not materially attractive to them. It seems improbable that all readers would consider any particular subject matter or technique to be invariably interesting.* But even if a

---

* The evaluation may of course be qualified: "This work will interest everyone who . . ." At the moment, however, we are attempting to discover whether any assertion of a value response can have unlimited and unconditional validity for all readers.

working agreement to an assumption about interest properties could be reached, the second objection is decisive. The reason for disapproving of the first line of analysis between data and appraisal was that it required the making of an assumption—for dogmatic, that is, unproved, definitions of literary value are necessarily assumptive. If the second line of analysis is also to involve us in assumptions, nothing will be gained by preferring it to the first. Not even the discovery of a working agreement will enable the critic to get rid of an assumptive element in his demonstration. A contingency will remain: the evidence will confirm the value judgment only so far as the assumption about interest properties is unconditionally sound.

The second illustrative hypothesis will differ from the first in short-cutting the identification of a specified value with particular value properties. If I assert that a poem achieves admirable rhythmic effects, I have again stated an evaluative proposition, for "admirable" describes a subjective response rather than an objective property. In attempting to corroborate the proposition I shall probably call attention to subtle variations of rhythmic emphasis, the adaptation of movement to meaning, the creation and resolution of metrical tensions, and so on. Unfortunately the former difficulty obtrudes itself again: What proof can I offer that these properties are an objective equivalent of the judgment "admirable rhythmic effects"? The proof (one may retort) that they have been widely admired; but so have the singsong of Edgar Guest and the thump-thump of Vachel Lindsay. I have conclusively demonstrated only that the poem contains subtle variations of emphasis, an adaptation of movement to meaning, and the rest. In strict logic, the analytical data which I have used as evidence for the appraisal are evidence of nothing but themselves. As J. M. Murry has remarked of truth, "Nothing is precious because it is true save to a mind which has, consciously or unconsciously, decided that it is good to know the truth."[13] I have made use of a preconceived standard of rhythmic qualities. My evaluative judgment is not demonstrated but is assumed.

Kaplan's explanation of the difficulties, which I have not quoted until now because of its technical idiom, is as follows:

> That X serves as evidence for Y rests ultimately on a causal connection between X and Y. Hence the appraisal is here construed as asserting (or predicting) the existence of a certain property (Y) causally connected with those taken as evidence for the appraisal. The difficulties are the same as in the first alternative: with what justification is the appraisal specified in terms of that particular Y? The appraisal of X in terms of its causal connection with Y depends on an appraisal of Y; and if appraisal is always in terms of such connection, the process is viciously regressive. The regress can be brought to an end only by *defining* a particular element as suitable endpoint. This is the first alternative, already rejected.[14]

Do such trains of reasoning seem farfetched and obscurantist? I am sure that to persons absorbed by the immediacies of experience they will. "What an unnecessary beating about of brains!" some readers may exclaim. "Can't everybody see that good literature is (or does) so-and-so?" I fear that not everybody can. Like political convictions, assumptions about literary value seem irrefutable precisely because they do not rest on evidence and therefore cannot be confuted by evidence. Like political convictions again, they lead to unfruitful controversy because the real grounds of difference are seldom brought into the open. The man who believes it unarguable that literature should do so-and-so is likely, in disputation, to devote his energy to the demonstration that a poem or novel meets unspecified conditions, with the result that his failure to convince opponents who assume different conditions leaves him perplexed and doubtful of human sanity. A remark by R. B. Perry is relevant.

There is a characteristic danger that attends any attempt to reach a new generalization, the danger, namely, of unconsciously assuming and employing the very concept which is under discussion ... Thus most of the traditional discussions of "the good" have in reality been attempts to discover that particular thing or those particular things that are good, instead of attempts to discover *what it means* for a thing to be good.[15]

The only way to avoid dissipation of energy and arrive finally at an understanding of the real grounds of difference is to undertake such abstract speculations as those in which we are engaged.

The third line of analysis construes the relationship between analytic data and appraisal as causal. The described facts effect an evaluative reaction, as Richards has said; the critic "calls attention to the facts so that their being perceived will produce in the percipient an appraisal which he might not otherwise have reached."[16]

Let us once again examine an illustrative instance. Analysis reveals that in *Paradise Lost* Milton constantly assumes a hierarchical organization of human (also, for that matter, of nonhuman) society. "How fine!" a critic like C. S. Lewis will reflect. "How exactly right! How thoroughly in harmony with the laws of God and nature!" Not all persons, however, will make this response. A critic with different sociological preconceptions will think, rather, "How disgusting! A reactionary view. We have got beyond *that*, at least." How can the difference of opinion be adjudicated?

It is evident that we cannot adjudicate between the evaluations without falling back on some other line of analysis. If we grant the causal relationship of the datum to the appraisal, as is essential to try the soundness of the argument, we must simply accept the fact that a single analytic finding has produced contrary evaluative reactions in two minds. The reactions are equally caused, and the theory suggests no way of preferring one to the other. Contrary preferences would in their turn be equally caused and hence equally valid. The process may be carried backward indefinitely without ever bringing us to a ground for logical discrimination. It becomes evident finally that the theory asserts nothing more than a kind of psychological determinism. The relationship between data and appraisal is not logical at all. There can be no such thing as a theory of criticism. There can only be psychoanalysis of critics.

The three lines of analysis are related, says Kaplan, to three major types of value theories, the first being dogmatic, the second scientific, or empirical, and the last impressionistic, or persuasive. None of the three views is acceptable to all the interested philosophers, and there seems to be no fourth possibility.[17] We are left with the sobering realization that from the point of view of strict logic there can be no such thing as a completely inductive value predication. Inductive analysis, yes—analysis leading to the perception of data which, although accepted into consciousness in patterns suited to the observing intelligence, are in a sense validly present in the literary subject matter. Values, on the contrary, seem not to be wholly *in* the literature and therefore are not discoverable through any analysis of the literature; or, if wholly in it, they are identifiable only by the aid of some arbitrary precommitment (as though the judges of a beauty contest were to decide before seeing the contestants that prizes would go to girls in orchid, apple-green, and canary-colored bathing suits). The behavioral qualities of evaluations are reasonably clear: we have perceptions and, at least in adulthood, recognize value properties almost simultaneously. But unless we are to prefer psychological explanations to logical ones or to accept as "logical" a judgment established by nose-counting, we seem to have reached an impasse. Analytical data are evaluatively neutral.[18] How, then, can we pass from analysis to judgment ("This poem is good or bad") or even to the assertion that it contains a specified value quality

("This poem is interesting, dull, delightful, contemptible, beautiful") with the assurance that we are not characterizing ourselves rather than the literature?

Only one course of action is open to us if we persist in wanting to arrive at predications about value that have a logical basis in the analytic findings. In spite of misgivings, we must fall back on the first line of analysis and accept the responsibility of defining value properties. The second and third lines of analysis either explode in our faces or lead in a roundabout way to the same conclusion as the first. "*Judgment of value*," writes Bertram Jessup, italicizing his words for emphasis, "*can be verified only by value, not by fact-simple* . . . In the phraseology of current slang it is always possible in the face of merely factual consequences to answer with factual finality, 'So what?' "[10] Only value facts have evaluative consequences. Facts-simple (analytic findings) have none. But the only value facts of relevance in this context are those specified by definitions of value, for only they can entail value predications on the basis of descriptive data.[20]

Our next step, consequently, must be to search for an acceptable definition of primary or quintessential literary value. We cannot hope to define all the conceivable value qualities—the nature of the "interesting," the "dull," the "charming," and the like—but if the character of the fundamental "good" in literature can somehow be pinned down and identified, we shall be able to make the discrimination that seems most to attract and tantalize critics, that between "good" literature and "bad."

9

Evaluation as Assumptive

THE TASK of defining primary or quintessential literary value is, unfortunately, perplexing in the extreme. The more steadily one looks at it the more formidable it appears. Where shall we search for the value—in literature only, or in the broader experience of which literature is merely a part? If in literature only, in what specific works? Goodness, clearly, can be discovered only in works which are good. If in all experience, how are we to find an adequate starting point for the train of reasoning which is to eventuate in the demarcation of a particular area of value as peculiarly literary?

Let us begin with the assumption that we wish to make an inductive approach. Almost immediately it becomes apparent that until we have defined the quintessential value it will be impossible to determine which of the world's writings contain it. We shall know where to look only after we have assumed an answer that will make further looking unnecessary. The situation is like that of a person unable to distinguish between fruits and other vegetables who is told to find out by investigation the basic nature of fruitiness: his mission requires the preliminary separating of fruits from nonfruits, but this he cannot accomplish without accepting on authority the very definition at which he is expected to arrive empirically.

The principle may be clarified by a literary illustration. Suppose that I am enamored of the idea that all speculative problems should be solved empirically. Let us get rid (I say to myself and preach to others) of *a priori* ideas, let us renounce all concern about where our investigation may lead us. Has not the inductive approach accomplished wonders in the physical and biological sciences? The time has come to be rigidly objective in literary criticism as in vertebrate anatomy and chemistry. The first of the great tasks awaiting the scientific critic is a sounder classification of genres. Was it not (I demand) by classifying plants that Linnaeus laid the foundations of modern botany? I will begin with poetry, the oldest of the literary media, and first will characterize the lyric, very possibly the oldest of all the poetic modes. With soaring hopes and eager empirical eyes I open the topmost of several scores of volumes arranged in piles round my desk and see the familiar title, "Sumer Is Icumen In." Excellent! I pull my typewriter toward me and begin rapidly to set down the words "A songlike rhythmic quality." Midway of the phrase, however, a doubt strikes me. How do I know that "Sumer Is Icumen In" is a lyric? If it is, well and good; but if not, its rhythmic qualities, songlike or other, are irrelevant to my quest.

In the last analysis, the question is answerable only by reference to a definition accepted, at least in its essentials, on authority. I turn to a handy dictionary and read, "having the form and musical quality of a song, and esp. the character of a songlike outpouring of the poet's own thoughts and feelings (as distinguished from *epic* and *dramatic* poetry, with their more extended and set forms and their presentation of external subjects)."[1] I have acquired a means of "proving" to myself and others that "Sumer Is Icumen In" is a lyric and therefore within the field I have undertaken to examine. But the proof is by authority; in my use, the definition is not empirical, and by accepting it I violate my profession of inductive methodology. More important still, if the limits of my inquiry are set by referring to the definition whenever the status of a poem is in doubt, my ultimate characterization of lyric poetry will include words equivalent to "having the form and musical quality of a song, and esp. the character of a songlike outpouring of the poet's own thoughts and feelings." It cannot be otherwise. I have admitted to investigation only poems which possess characteristics defined in advance, and hence the investigation will necessarily reveal the defined characteristics to be present. At most, I can discover that these characteristics are accompanied by others not a part of the original definition (and, I may argue, more important). In no event can I find the original definition to have been fundamentally in error. I have not, therefore, made much headway. The chances are very strong that I will end essentially where I began.

Recognition of the principle implicit in the foregoing illustration is disheartening. "Definitions are the ultimate basis of judgments of value"[1]—this is the knowledge at which we arrived in the last chapter. But "definitions regularly involve an arbitrary factor."[2] If this is so, how can value judgments ever stand firmly on empirical ground? The dilemma is summarized by R. B. Perry as follows:

> According to the empirical method, we are not to start with a category and then find instances of it, but must proceed in the reverse direction, first collecting instances and then analyzing out their common characteristic. In collecting instances, however, one has to employ a principle of selection; which will turn out, unless one is cautious, to be an assumption of the very concept of which one is supposed to be in search.[4]

Unless one is cautious. Again and again, in recent years, philosophers have tried patiently to learn what kind of caution will permit assurance that the definitional process is not circular. Stephen Pepper, for instance, in *The Basis of Criticism in the Arts*, suggested the use of triadic definitions in which the verbal symbol is made responsible both to an object or field of objects and to a detailed description of the objects;[5] but the thesis of the book is that the four major philosophies of our day suggest four different definitions of aesthetic value, each of which can be proved only by a train of reasoning that

88

rests ultimately on a root metaphor.[5] Bertram Jessup has recommended "inspectional" definitions: "theory addressing itself to [a] given field of facts can eliminate some and perhaps add others—but not too many either way."[6] Lewis Hahn agrees with Jessup (and Pepper) that in a discussion of value one must take as "a rough common-sense starting point the kinds of things philosophers, economists, and others interested in theory of value have been writing about for the past fifty years," but points out that different theorists "cite different areas of fact as the significant ones."[8] A doubt accordingly arises: How can we be sure that the facts Jessup would allow us to eliminate are not of special importance or that those he would allow us to add may not later develop a major and determinant character? In either event the results of the inspection will have been prejudiced. One concludes, rather sorrowfully, that no sure way has yet been found of delimiting a field of inquiry empirically, therefore no way of guaranteeing completely objective induction. What will be found depends on where we decide to look, and the decision about where to look is always in some degree arbitrary.

The unphilosophical tendency—common among critics, as among other people—is to disregard such reflections and rest in an intuitive certainty. Critics may "know" the truth about quintessential literary value without having to engage in reflection at all, or may be able to justify intuitive notions by reflections which appear to them immediately upon formulation to be self-evident. Now I have no wish to anger or depress persons who feel cozily secure among their beliefs, and I am perfectly willing to admit, for their comfort, that an intuition may be as "true" as the result of a long process of reasoning. Nevertheless, the precommitments of the present study require us to disallow convictions of a wholly irrational nature, and the self-evidence of justificatory reasoning is likely to be the effect of a vicious circularity. I may quote Perry on this point also.

It not infrequently happens that self-evidence arises from ambiguous redundancy. The redundancy creates an aspect of truth, while the ambiguity creates an aspect of importance. Thus if happiness means the same as what would satisfy if one had it, then it is safe to say that all men desire happiness; for this would then be no more than to say that all men desire that which they desire.[9]

I suspect, though I shall not attempt to demonstrate, that the self-evidence of propositions is due to concealed redundancy whenever it is not due to the psychological conditioning of the perceiver (as a boy reared in a minister's home may all his life resonate either positively or negatively to moral dogmas). But at any rate no definition of primary literary value advanced in our time has appeared self-evident to more than the members of a coterie, and coterie presumptions are necessarily unsatisfactory to the general theorist.

In practice every "empirical" searcher for quintessential literary value must resolve the difficulty we have been confronting by making whatever assumption about the field of inquiry seems to him least objectionable or methodologically most convenient. Thus one man may elect to take his stand upon the generally admitted, the indisputable, the commonly agreed on—such works as the *Iliad*, the *Aeneid*, the *Divine Comedy*, *Hamlet*, *Tartuffe*, and *Faust*. His choices are not likely to win unanimous approval—T. S. Eliot, for example, has announced *Hamlet* to be "most certainly an artistic failure"[10]—and his conclusions will be questionable in proportion as his materials are scanty. Nevertheless, he has made an honest effort to limit the field inductively as well as to start his exploration of it without preconceptions, and his assumption, that literary value is best estimated by a kind of universal vote subject to constant review, is at least respectable. Another man, feeling that he needs a larger number of documents with which to work, might conceivably go through the writings of all the critics in whose good taste he confides and rule to be "good" the creative works mentioned by several with obvious approval. The assumption here is that the critics deferred to are trustworthy guides. A third man may decide after long perplexity that he cannot do better than to recognize validity in his own strong emotional preferences. This delimitation of the field is of course subjective, but all experience is subjective on one level; the critics in whom the second man placed confidence felt subjectively the approval they later set down in ink symbols. The field of inquiry must always be delimited by reference to some authority, that of other people or of one's own intuition, and will yield results no more reliable than the chosen authority itself.

It is possible, also, to abandon empirical methods, start from another direction, and settle the nature of primary literary value by deductions from other items of speculative belief—for example, a philosophy of aesthetics. More will be said about aesthetic definitions in a following chapter. At present it is necessary only to observe that the description of literary value will then be contingent on the truth of the propositions to which it is corollary; and the proof of those propositions will at some point involve the acceptance of an assumption. All reasoning, one comes gradually to see, is reasoning in a circle. At some point every argument turns back on itself. An ontology may generate an epistemology, the epistemology a logic, the logic and epistemology in combination an aesthetics, and cognitive data obtained through the aesthetics may finally be used to verify the ontology. There exists, in fact, no criterion of truth but the coherence criterion. In the last analysis every human belief is tested against other beliefs.[11] Even the appeal to perceptions, which is final in physical science, assumes the trustworthiness of the senses, which in turn is justified by the results attainable through the assumption.

These conclusions are supported by an examination of value definitions actually stated or implied by practicing critics. However plausible the definition may sound, however deftly it may pretend to self-sufficiency, a little scrutiny reveals its dependence on other notions which are either themselves assumptive or rest on assumptions at one or more removes.

Let us look, for instance, at the fairly widespread belief, noted by Mark Schorer, that vividness and complexity are literary values.[12] The view is highly intelligent, since it is in harmony with the dominant American philosophy, contextualism (as an elaborated pragmatism has recently begun to be called). For the very reason that it is derivative from a philosophy, however, it is impugnable. Contextualism is not certainly the "correct" philosophy or even certainly the "best" of those now living and vigorous. Other world hypotheses offer equally adequate descriptions of the universe of experience. The definitions of aesthetic—and also, by extension or adaptation, of literary—value given by philosophers of other schools do not support but compete with the contextualistic definition. A mechanistic aesthetician like Santayana may find value in a completely undifferentiated texture and is likely to deny aesthetic value to the vividly ugly. No proof of the "truthfulness" of the contextualistic world view has so far succeeded in silencing opposition, nor is it likely to do so in the future. If contextualism at length prevails over other world views, the reason will be that it has been found, like Copernican astronomy, to have a preëminent analytic convenience.

Many judicial assumptions used even by unphilosophical critics are related to philosophical thought currents. For instance, the fairly common opinion that literature is praiseworthy if it completely realizes the author's intention is appropriate to the Crocean theory of art as expression. The valuing of representative qualities ("Tennyson's poetry reflects the preoccupation of nineteenth-century Englishmen with moral ideals") would seem to have connections with formism. But some definitions are more or less independent of philosophical thought, and these are more immediately and naïvely assumptive. For example, Trollope, in the critical chapters of his *Autobiography*, reveals by indirection that his criterion of prose fiction is lifelike character portrayal rather than the *utile miscere dulci* principle he believes himself to hold.[13] He assumes, that is to say, that novelists ought to people their books with persons like those the reader sees about him in everyday existence. Good reasons could be given for the assumption (if pursued, it would probably lead again to formism), but Trollope was no philosopher, and his acceptance of the standard was probably due to nothing more than a temperamental readiness to respond emotionally to almost any kind of immediate human situation. He needed no poetical heightening.

In sum, no definition of literary value carries absolute authority. As Dashiell has said, "It seems as if the determination of the philosophical status of anything inevitably starts from some limited type of philosophy";[14] and no status can be more authoritative than a philosophical one, for philosophy is simply human thought carried as far as it can go. The most fully articulated and exhaustively investigated theories of value "carry with them immediate implications about the nature of Reality. They are, indeed, primarily asseverations about the nature, or an aspect of the nature, of Reality."[15] But all theories about reality are working hypotheses, not demonstrated truths. The theologian conceives of reality in one set of terms, the philosopher in another, the physicist in a third, the man in the street in a fourth. In the reasoning of each there is somewhere an ultimate category of ideas which is primary, unanalyzable, and therefore assumptive.

Does it follow that we should not attempt the evaluation of literary documents? By no means. Life is full of choices, and we have as good reason to judge literature as to express opinions about other matters that concern us. One may properly insist, however, that the professional critic choose his definition of primary literary value with care. The teacher, especially, who in the course of a single working day often speaks evaluatively of many literary works to students whose minds may be lastingly impressed by his opinions, can well afford to expend some pains in the establishment of his evaluative criterion instead of relying on arbitrary and unanalyzed intuitive presumptions.

10

Orders of Evaluative Assumptions

IN ITS DETAILS, the establishment of a definition of literary value is the responsibility of the individual critic, who can feel certainties denied to the more impartial theorist. For every man some ideas are absolutely valid, some principles so necessary for the meaningfulness of experience that when they are admitted to fall into doubt the universe becomes chaos. The general theorist, however, is bound by the logical aspects of things; and since it has already become clear that every definition of value is in some degree alogical he cannot give an unqualified preference to any single definition. The most he can do is to describe some of the large orders of assumptions and comment briefly on their differences. In metaphorical terms, he can merely try to find one or more natural boundaries dividing the speculative area and characterize as helpfully as possible the sections into which the area appears to fall.

The boundaries that the literary theorist will discover are not those that would seem most significant to the philosopher. The philosopher's eye is alert for a different order of phenomena—geological, so to speak, not botanical. The questions for which the literary critic wishes answers are relatively specific. He is not likely to ask, In what terms can the general concept "value" best be construed? What is the locus of value—the object, the human percipient, or a situation including both? Are value judgments propositions or emotive ejaculations? These and similar problems, which have importance for the philosopher, will probably be dismissed by the practical critic as outside his province. I shall be much mistaken if the practical critic does not wish chiefly to know what kinds of evaluative assumptions can be made intelligently. Once he has been informed about the kinds, he can choose, or abstain from choosing, among them on whatever grounds he is accustomed to use in making speculative decisions.

Since the attitude of the philosopher toward the ultimate problems of value is more serious than that of the critic, in the long run the philosopher will no doubt reach sounder conclusions. Any definition of literary value offered now is liable to modification in the comparatively near future in the light of new discoveries by value theorists. No useful purpose, however, would be served by confronting the deeper issues here. In the absence of substantial agreement about how the issues are to be resolved, the discussion would ramify formidably. It will be best to make a single dichotomous division of a kind suited to clarify fundamental preferences and then to develop each of the rival views as adequately as space permits. After all, the critic must cut off his examination of theory at some point so as to return to his proper activities. With relation to the general theory of value, he is in the position of the farmer who, instead of performing his own experiments in poultry breeding, must await the publication of a definitive pamphlet by the Department of Agriculture, and in the meantime must set his hens in accordance with theories not yet known to be unsound.

The most helpful dichotomy is that between aesthetic and not wholly aesthetic definitions. Literature may be judged as art and nothing but art, or it may be considered as partly art and partly something else. That is to say, it may be assumed that good writing has a responsibility only to beauty, or that it has a responsibility also to truth or morality, or both.

The divergencies of critical opinion resulting from different choices between the alternatives are immense and probably unbridgeable in terms of particulars. For example, how can a man whose reaction to Proust's À la

Recherche du temps perdu is, "What beautiful composition!" communicate with a man whose reaction is, "How morally diseased!" No amount of discussion can bring the two to agree on an evaluation as long as they confine their remarks to the literary work itself. Each could admit the validity of the other's comment without feeling in the least constrained to depart from his own evaluative judgment. There is no common ground, hence no real issue, except, of course, that the first man probably believes himself to have said "How good!" and the second "How bad!" Both have stated appraisals in what they thought were appropriate terms, but the two universes of discourse overlap only enough to make discussion confusing. The first critic has assumed literature to have a responsibility only to art, whereas the second has assumed it to have a responsibility also to morality.

The former of the two views derives from a feeling that the essence of literature is not touched by discussion of it as anything but art. At the present time, says David Daiches,

> [criticism] is serving several functions—psychological, sociological, political, ethical, even metaphysical—and in so far as it serves these functions adequately it is valuable, but when criticism fulfilling any or all of these functions masquerades indiscriminately as "literary" the resulting confusion is overwhelming. The sociologist will find a value in Dickens, the psychologist a value in Shakespeare, the feminist a value in Meredith, and other specialists will find other values in the same writers. But literary worth is distinct—even if, as some hold, it is composite.[1]

Again, in a later work, "to judge fiction as fiction is very difficult, while to judge it as history, sociology, or rhetoric is fairly easy. We all tend to take the line of least resistance."[2]

A great many students of literature must have had similar reflections. Scott's novels have considerable historical accuracy—but what bearing has that fact on my complete coldness to them? Ezra Pound is a fascist; very well, but some of his short poems are delightful. After much perplexity about the essential meaninglessness of many discoveries about literature that *seem* important, one may conclude that the discoveries are irrelevant because they are extraliterary. What, then, is literature? The reply may come finally, "It is a form of art, like music and painting; therefore criticism must discuss it as art." A consequence of this decision is that critical methodology becomes aesthetic.

Unfortunately, the science of aesthetics is harder to pin down than such a science as physics or zoölogy. The characterization of a beautiful sonnet in half a dozen textbooks of elementary aesthetics would probably vary in a way not paralleled by a characterization of frogs or dogfish in half a dozen textbooks of elementary zoölogy. The reason is that in aesthetics there is as yet no complete agreement, as for a long time there has been in zoölogy, about the point of view an investigator must take. Every aesthetician has a choice of preliminary assumptions, and thence proceeds along whatever course seems to him dialectically soundest to whatever conclusions most commend themselves to his reason and emotions.

The absence of a body of formulated and generally accepted data makes it very difficult to summarize the implications for criticism of an aesthetic definition of literary value. It is impossible to discuss *the* aesthetic standard for literature, since none has strong predominance. The only feasible course of action is to offer a brief explanation of major emphases.

The most sharply drawn analysis of current emphases (we may disregard those of merely historical importance) seems to be that of Stephen Pepper, who, in *The Basis of Criticism in the Arts,* analyzes the aesthetic systems appropriate to four living philosophies which appear to give about equally adequate explanations of the universe of experience. I shall lean heavily on this analysis, supplying, however, my own explanations of the systems and introducing a secondary classification of which Professor Pepper might not approve.

Aesthetic definitions of literary value usually stress either the formal properties of art or the ability of art works to evoke sensations. Definitions of the former kind are suitable to organistic and formistic philosophies; definitions of the latter, to mechanistic and contextualistic philosophies.[3]

The classic statement of the organistic view is Bosanquet's *Three Lectures on Aesthetic*. This view requires of beauty an organic unity similar to that believed by organicists to obtain in the universe as a whole. Every detail in the perfect art work calls for the presence of every other; nothing is lacking, nothing is unnecessary; everything coalesces into the whole, the supremely neat and workmanlike whole. In criticizing fiction, writes Percy Lubbock, we have nothing to say until the author announces his subject.

> But from that moment he is accessible, his privilege is shared; and the delight of treating the subject is acute and perennial. From point to point we follow the writer, always looking back to the subject itself in order to understand the logic of the course he pursues. We find that we are creating a design, large or small, simple or intricate, as the chapter finished is fitted into its place; or again there is a flaw and a break in the development, the author takes a turn that appears to contradict or to disregard the subject, and the critical question, strictly so called, begins ... So it goes, till the book is ended and we look back at the whole design.[4]

A "good" work, then, is one in which the design is adequate to the subject and completely harmonious with itself; a "bad" work has disharmonies, unresolved contradictions, materials lacking or in surplus. The difference between art and nonart, the beautiful and the not-beautiful, praiseworthy literature and literature which lacks merit, is to be sought in the details of construction.

The structural expectations of the formist differ from those of the organicist in permitting a narrower range of variation. The organicist's eye is always on completeness, roundness, reciprocation; to his mind the achievement of fused unity justifies any choice of techniques. The formist, on the other hand, insists on a certain deference to the usual ways of doing things, not necessarily because he is intellectually timid but because he sees value in normality, which tends to receive the approval of many judges. To the formist, traditional structures seem better than idiosyncratic ones because experience has proved them to have a natural fitness for the representation of normal human experience. In a manner of speaking, literature wants to be written in forms sanctioned by the community and resents being twisted into forms congenial only to individual talents. The straining of art toward norms is explained as consequent on the fact that nature is not continuous but discontinuous. Like the table of chemical elements (I borrow the illustration from Pepper), nature contains stable resting places separated by gaps which only unstable organizations can occupy. Authors ought to seek out and use the stable literary forms precisely as a man who must mount a ladder ought to feel for the rungs and not put his feet in the interstices. Thus the sonnet, once invented, proved to be the ideal medium for the expression of a certain range of poetic emotions. Moreover, the laws of each of the stable structures can be established rather accurately by induction (*vide* the method of Aristotle's *Poetics*, the most celebrated of formistic documents). The sonnet, for example, usually falls into two parts, the general and the specific; two rhyme schemes predominate in English; there are often rhythmical breaks at certain points; the tone is regularly confessional; and so on. The formist's appraisals, accordingly, turn on such ideas as those of genre, mimesis, and universality.

The aesthetics of sensation or feeling differs from that of structure in stressing the relationship between the art object and a percipient subject (and therefore is particularly liable to the problems of subjectivity). It has already been observed that for the mechanist there may be value in an undifferentiated texture—let us say that of a piece of velvet cloth not sewed into any pattern and therefore virtually without form. The taste of a pear or a slice of cold beef may seem to him aesthetically enjoyable, whereas the organicist ought properly to believe that such unconstructed tastes lie outside the aesthetic field. The point at issue is whether the artist's craftsmanship or the perceiver's feeling response is primary in aesthetic judgment. The answer returned to the question by the mechanist and contextualist requires that their definitions of aesthetic value be distinguished rather sharply from those of the organicist and the formist.

The motive behind the stressing of response becomes apparent if we remember the possibility of giving intellectual approval to works of literary (or other) art toward which we feel emotionally indifferent. "Yes, that's good," we may say, recognizing craftsmanship of an indubitably high order; but only compulsion could make us turn to the work a second time. The mechanist resolves this ambiguity of attitude by urging that the function of art is to give pleasure. Formal qualities are important to him only so far as they conduce to enjoyment, and whatever gives enjoyment without analyzable form has aesthetic value notwithstanding. A tantalizing perfume, the exhilarating bite of sea air, the murmur of wind among leaves, although not art, by stimulating the senses agreeably falls within the range of aesthetics; and human constructs like literature are aesthetically "good" in proportion as they evoke pleasurable sensations. "Not the fruit of experience," wrote Walter Pater in the famous conclusion to his *Renaissance*, "but experience itself, is the end. A counted number of pulses only is given to us of a variegated, dramatic life." Art is important because it can help us to "be present always at the focus where the greatest number of vital forces unite in their purest energy."

The contextualist also prizes sensory vividness, but is less insistent than the mechanist that the vividness be immediately pleasurable. To the contextualist, preëminently, art appears to be a form of knowledge, a mode of sensory cognition, a way of apprehending experience directly instead of through the medium of the discursive reason. Accordingly he feels that it is perceptions of quality, the feel of situations, which art is peculiarly fitted to communicate. The quality of a thundershower can be expressed more vividly by a poem than by a meteorological report; the quality of a marital quarrel, by a short story than by a syllogistic analysis; the quality of a war, by a novel than by a compilation of communiqués and logistics records. As sentient human beings we are quite as much concerned with the surface of experience as with the "factual" realities, physical, chemical, structural, and statistical, which underlie the surface. Water is a taste, a spectacle, a tactual sensation, and sometimes a sound, as well as a combination of hydrogen and oxygen in the proportion of two to one; and for consciousness the sensory qualities are quite as important as the chemical. The function of art is to do what other modes of expression do less effectively: to communicate sensory knowledge. The contextualistic measure of literary value has therefore been said to be the vividness and breadth of the perceptual experience initiated in the reader.[5]

The aesthetic emphases we have been considering have relevance to criticism only so far as literature is art. For several pages we have been assuming it to be wholly art; and certainly a fairly large number of contemporary critics seem to imply that it is nothing else. Excellent arguments can be offered in justification of their practice. For example, as what, if not as art, do we enjoy Aeschylus' *The Eumenides,* Virgil's description of Hades, or, perhaps, even Bunyan's *Pilgrim's Progress?* "No crash of systems," wrote William Vaughan Moody of *Paradise*

Lost in his edition of Milton's poetry, "can drown its noble music." The music of literature, its sound, its imagery, its contagious feeling, its form, can continue to give satisfaction when the ideas that are partly responsible for its coherence seem quaint and perhaps despicable. Nevertheless, there has never been, possibly never will be, agreement among critics that literature ought always to be discussed in purely aesthetic terms.

The resistance to exclusively aesthetic standards of judgment can be explained by the fact that syntactical combinations of words can rarely avoid altogether the expression of ideas, and ideas can be criticized in their own right as valid or invalid formulations or evaluations of experience. A sonata or vase can approach pure form to a degree that even the purest lyric poem cannot. Something is usually said or implied by literature about the universe of everyday life—something that can be considered apart from the manner of the saying, something that can be appraised independently. More technically, literature may be thought insufficiently congruent with the other arts to fall entirely within the scope of general aesthetics. Certain aspects of it may be thought to fall outside the aesthetic field—aspects which can be disregarded only at the expense of forfeiting the claim to total appraisal.

This position has been argued recently with regard to poetry, in the *Journal of Aesthetics and Art Criticism;*[6] but the current tendency to discuss art in terms merely of form, texture, and sensation is opposed to a philosophical tradition of long standing. Samuel Alexander spoke in the tradition when he said, "The greater art is concerned more extensively, more profoundly and more subtly with the main tendencies in human nature and in things." For Alexander, adequate form and design sufficed only to place an object within the class of beautiful (aesthetic) objects; its rank within the class depended on subject matter or content.[7] The direct application to literature of a similar principle was made by the French literary theorist Ricardou in the very work in which he urged that scientific criticism ought to be aesthetic and not historical. "A literary work," he said in one of several formulations of his own evaluative criterion, "is more beautiful in proportion as it expresses more truth and morality in a more impressive form."[8] Literature overlaps the three speculative areas of the good, the true, and the beautiful and is fractured when discussed in terms of form and texture only. Henry Osborn Taylor declared that "The function of art . . . is to give utterance and form to the content of human life—thought, action, conviction, feeling, emotion—and to the setting, the natural environment, in which humanity acts and thinks and feels."[9] Critics with more modest philosophical pretensions have also many times stated analogous opinions. Thus Daiches, a professor of literature, argues—it seems to me—more cogently on this side of the aesthetic-nonaesthetic dichotomy than on the other:

> The critic must see literature as one of numerous activities, otherwise what function has he at all? . . . The critic is the link between the work of art and the world, and his duty is to determine their relation. The nature of literary value is dependent on the nature of the relation of art to the whole of life, and to attempt to pass judgment on literature without having come to some conclusion regarding this relation can have no useful result, because it means assessing value on an undetermined criterion.[10]

J. M. Murry, a journalistic critic, points out that many things besides art have been required of poetry: "Delight, music, subtlety of thought, a world of the heart's desire, fidelity to comprehensible experience, a glimpse through magic casements, profound wisdom."[11] The ordinary periodical reviewer rarely discusses literature solely as art; and the man in the street, whose reading is limited to an occasional novel or biography, would perhaps be astonished to learn of the possibility that literature might be so discussed.

104

From the most sophisticated levels of thought to the least sophisticated, from the most abstract to the most concrete, the view that a "good" literary work must have more than an adequate form and texture finds support. This does not mean that the view is necessarily "correct." I dwell on its intellectual respectability only because in recent years there has been a growing tendency, especially among "new" critics, to regard as stupid and tiresome any criticism which refuses to grant an author his right to hold even the wildest opinions about life and the universe.

To judge from their writings, some nonaesthetic critics go so far as to deny any importance whatever to literary artistry. Marxist critics have often been accused of following a party line, of judging literature solely with reference to political and sociological implications. The charge is probably false; nevertheless, such a work as Upton Sinclair's *Mammonart*—if it is Marxist—gives some color to the accusation. Jeremy Collier's *A Short View of the Profaneness and Immorality of the English Stage,* an influential document of the late seventeenth century, is concerned chiefly with the morality of stage situations. A psychological critic may speak of a novel in glowing terms because it illustrates the possibility of adjusting to apparently intolerable social circumstances. Businessmen engaged in merchandising and clergymen who preach a doctrine of confident living seem to approve of any work which says, like the title of Betty MacDonald's recent book, *Anybody Can Do Anything.* It is probable, however, that all critics whose writings have much meaning for the readers of these pages would admit, if pressed, that literature has aesthetic responsibilities. The purpose of arguing a limited nonaesthetic thesis (as that Coleridge was a pious hypocrite) is not meant to imply a total condemnation (that none of Coleridge's poetry or prose has aesthetic value). At most, the denial of a specific nonliterary virtue to a work is intended to refute the work's claim to a particular kind of essential goodness. For this reason I have distinguished between criticism which is wholly aesthetic and that which is only partly so, instead of making a triadic division among aesthetic, partly aesthetic, and nonaesthetic criticism. Except in the preceding sentence, indeed, the word "nonaesthetic" has been used here as equivalent to "not wholly aesthetic." Few persons whose interest in literature is not wholly derivative from an interest in something else will believe that literature has none of the properties of art and hence can be judged solely with reference to standards drawn from politics, ethics, or sociology.

If, then, literature is granted to have nonaesthetic as well as aesthetic responsibilities, how is it possible to arrive at a definition of literary value which will permit the characterization of individual works as "good" or "bad"?

The question is complex—so complex that an attempt to reply to it in other than the most abstract terms would ramify beyond control. An adequate answer would require, first, the division of the whole realm of logical discourse into a number of distinct areas; next, the specification of areas into which literature projects; and finally, the determination of exactly what properties or qualities discoverable in each area a literary work must possess in order to fulfill all its responsibilities. If it were decided that "good" literature must be at once moral and true and beautiful, the appraisal of a given work as good would require the preliminary establishment of definitions of morality and truth as well as beauty. But how are such definitions to be established? By a repetition of the processes through which we have gone in considering possible definitions of aesthetic value. Every ethical system—to follow out only one-half of the illustrative hypothesis—is adequate only from a particular point of view, with relation only to one configuration of extra-ethical thought. Evidently a determination to define ethical value would force us a second time to examine a whole series of alternative theories, organistic, formistic, mechanistic, and contextualistic. A similar process would then have to be repeated a third time in order to establish a criterion of truth. It is very likely, however, that the Platonic triad of speculative fields is not suited to modern thought. If it is not, some other schematization of knowledge than the traditional one of the good, the true, and the beautiful would have to be worked out, the connection of literary value with each area somehow decided, and an inclusive definition of all the value properties essential to good literature formulated.

The task may well appear monstrous. If the critic decides, in desperation, to fall back on the first and apparently simpler line of analysis, he will learn that the attempt to separate nonaesthetic experience from aesthetic is an almost equally exhausting discipline. One ought not to say, "Only this kind of experience is aesthetic," without first taking pains to learn how great is the range of possible experience and how all nonaesthetic experiences can best be categorized. The pains will lead the responsible aesthetician far afield before he reaches his conclusions. The truth is that on every vital world hypothesis except the formistic the entire universe of experience is one closely woven texture. Life is not a carved Indian ball of separately revolving spheres, but rather an incredibly huge and tangled skein of yarn. If we pull long enough on any strand we will come at last to all the others; and no piece can be torn free without some injury both to it and to the remainder.

Again we seem to have reached a logical impasse. The ultimate goal of criticism, it was decided in chapter 1, is a full, evaluated apprehension of the critical subject matter. But it quickly became apparent (in chap. 2) that a full apprehension of even the shortest and most trivial work is impossible. The critic must make a choice, must direct his efforts to the obtaining of whatever kinds of accessible knowledge he decides are most precious to him (chaps. 3, 5, 6, 7). We then shifted our attention to evaluation and discovered that value is a matter of definition only (chap. 8), and that all definitions are assumptive (chap. 9). Now we see that an attempt to explore the grounds of alternative assumptions which permit total evaluation leads us from the study of literature into a study of everything under and above the sun—in theory, at least, ought so to lead us.

Is there any way out? Can we resolve this second dilemma, as we resolved the first, by modifying our expectations? This is the question to be considered in the final chapter.

11

The Choice among Assumptions

ONE WAY of meeting the situation is to confess defeat and retire, if possible in good order, but with standards discreetly lowered. We can renounce any hope of attaining half of the theoretical goal (a full, evaluated apprehension of the critical subject matter) and expend our energies on the effort merely to sharpen and deepen our apprehensions.

There is nothing unintelligent about such a decision. On the contrary, only the unusually astute critic is aware that by revealing a trait he has not proved a judgment but has only—revealed the trait. It is the failure to recognize a logical gulf between analytic findings and appraisals that now appears to be intellectually naïve. Moreover, there is a kind of generosity, a kind of amiability, in the willingness to spread out discoveries for anybody's taking, without stipulation about how they must be used. It is as though the reader were told, "Things are what they are, but your soul is your own." And, finally, it would be a mistake to see timidity in every abstention from judgment. Critics may sometimes withhold evaluations through fear of challenging disagreement. For the most part, however, the hesitation to judge is motivated by the hope of achieving competence in a special investigative area. The critic thinks of himself as a "scholar" or "literary historian" and in his own mind defines his purposes in such a way as to have no responsibility to evaluate.

Why, indeed, should there not be specialization in criticism as well as elsewhere? The qualitative difference between analysis and appraisal is quite as sharp as that between orthopedics and dermatology or between carpentry and plumbing. Nobody criticizes the physician who sets a broken femur for not at the same time treating the patient for athlete's foot, or the carpenter who leaves a plumbing outlet in the bathroom wall for not trying to hammer a pipe into it. The analogy is less than exact; one might better draw a comparison with the orthopedist's assumption that once the leg is healed the patient will walk wherever he wishes on it, or the carpenter's readiness to let his employer fill a completed cabinet with either dishes or jam pots. At any rate, the separation of the total critical process into two parts is not arbitrary, as would be the carpenter's determination to lay boards only north and south or the orthopedist's to set only left femurs.

All this is not to say that abstention from judgment is necessarily praiseworthy. Neutrality may be, no doubt sometimes is, the result of emotional doltishness—an inability to respond to literature vigorously enough to permit the question of values to arise. The grounds for believing that every coolly analytical essay has been kept impartial only by a tremendous effort at self-control are not very solid. It is difficult to run one's eye over the bibliographies in scholarly handbooks without suspecting that the authors of many of the listed writings had little real interest in literature. The suspicion is once again awakened that some scholarly studies are the work of persons who became trapped in departments of literature by accident and, once irrevocably there, felt it necessary to establish themselves in the profession by writing essays on whatever topics were within their scope. In depressed moods one may even wonder whether it is not precisely such displaced persons who have set the temper and established the critical methodology of our scholarly journals. Nevertheless, one should make a strong effort not to sink into a mood of uncharitable asperity. Serenity may be achieved as well as imposed by a phlegmatic nature, and the suspension of judgment may be due to a high and pure ideal of scientific objectivity.

If impartiality is impossible or emotionally discomforting, the critic can obtain some relief by stating partial evaluations. "This work," he may declare, "is in such-and-such a way admirable": its composition is excellent, its sociological implications salutary, its style prepossessing, or some other property or quality "good." There is risk in such pronouncements, but less than in flat assertions that works are good or bad in their entirety.

The risk is less because compositional skill, salutary social implications, prepossessing style, and other isolated aspects of literature are, first, less complex than the concept of total goodness or badness, and, second, are less likely to provoke bitter controversy. They are less complex because they are only a part of a whole and necessarily contain less than the whole. This is not to say that they are simple or yield readily to analysis. One need only look at the phrase "salutary social implications" to realize how tremendously complicated they can be. Fortunately, however—and this observation brings us to the second point—it is often possible to arrive at tentative agreements for the sake of permitting specific discussions. Thus the explanation that an admirable style is a style which is well suited to the expression of the author's subject may be accepted without vigorous protest. Though the definition is arbitrary, it does not prick the average reader in a tender spot as an arbitrary definition of total literary value might. The reader can probably grant the critic the reference frame and the appropriate evaluative conclusion without compromising any settled judgments that he holds dear. In a word, partial appraisals are fairly safe because they are made on a level below that on which the most stubborn clashes of opinion occur. Acquiescence comes reasonably cheap. Yet the critic who has argued the thesis may obtain considerable satisfaction from establishing it, for to him it may appear that what he has said about the work is the single thing most worth saying.

It may be argued plausibly that evaluation need never

go further than this. What matters about a literary work, it may be urged, is not its value but its values. There is never any necessity to compare, to rate, to establish scales. Let the critic draw out (*evaluate*) the work's special qualities. Let him call attention to the satisfactions it is able to impart, or the desires it will frustrate, or both. Beyond this he has no responsibility to go. There is no need to sum up, to give A's and B's and F's like a pedagogue grading a student's paper.

The point is well taken, and I should myself be happy to grant it. In the present study, however, we are committed by a study of prevailing opinion to a broader view of the critical goal. The person who wishes to press toward a *full*, evaluated apprehension of the work he has undertaken to scrutinize will be gratified but not satisfied by the acquisition of a handful of value facts. He will want to learn whether the work is valuable as a whole, and how it is to be judged comparatively.

The question throws us back upon all the difficulties involved in defining total or quintessential literary goodness. The risks are greater than those involved in non-evaluative analysis or in the returning of partial appraisals—greater even than the sum of the risks taken in making a series of partial appraisals, for an additional assumption is made in equating total value with a complex of admittedly partial values. The wish may none the less persevere, and, from the point of view basic to the present study, must be granted to be honorable.

One bit of preliminary advice, at least, may be offered. The critic who insists on returning total judgments ought in all reason honestly to acknowledge his standards, to define his understanding of total literary value either expressly or by unmistakable implication. If he does not, his appraisals will lack a frame of reference and therefore will be meaningless to readers who look to criticism for rational and not emotive demonstration. If not related to evaluative principle as well as to literary fact, the exclamation "I approve!" or "I condemn!" will float beautifully, perhaps, but unsubstantially far above the head of the earth-walker, who may yearn after it as he yearns after the beauty he feels in creative literature, but will sigh at the realization that his hope of arriving at responsible knowledge has not been served.

One must not be unreasonable. The fondness of many critics for indirect statement (arising, no doubt, from whatever psychic traits make them prefer poems, plays, and novels to straightforward exposition) does not always veil their standards inscrutably. When a critic like Arnold or Eliot says of a few quoted verses "How fine!" or "How deplorable!" the acute reader can usually make fairly confident guesses about the standards of judgment. Nevertheless, clear advantages can be seen in the explicit avowal of value definitions. For one thing, the concealing of premises is wasteful of the reader's attention, which must often be diverted, if real understanding is sought, from what is said to the undivulged reasons for saying it. Again, one would think it useful to the critic to be aware of the assumptions underlying his opinions. Most important of all, the practice of avowing frames of evaluative reference would clarify discussions of value exactly as the custom of announcing an analytic point of view has increased the usefulness of the nonevaluative criticism published in academic journals.

The last point is worth dwelling on briefly. Present critical habits conduce to the sharp posing of interpretive, but not of evaluative, issues. Here, for example, are the introductory sentences from an article published recently in an academic journal:

> We shall be concerned with the exposition of three pairs of James' key critical words: action and character, register and centre, and scene and picture. The citations will be drawn mainly from the critical prefaces to the New York edition and the collateral references mainly from his later fictions, since it is the mature theory and practice in which we are interested.[1]

Nothing could be more explicit. The reader is told that the critical terms, of which there are no more than six, will be studied with reference to two related bodies of material, all other sources of information being played down; A is to be examined from points of view X and Y. Contrast with this clarity the confusion that attended a famous attack made on Milton's style by T. S. Eliot, who only after some decades was understood to have meant chiefly that "the contemporary situation is such . . . that Milton is a master whom [modern poets] should avoid."[2] The instances are by no means extreme. Except when decision is contingent on a lost bit of historical information, interpretive issues tend to be cleared up rather quickly, whereas evaluative issues drag on until one of the disputants is forced to acknowledge his X.

The confusion is avoidable. All that is necessary is general recognition that "criticism" as well as "scholarship" should be responsible to a declared point of view. At present there are few signs of such a recognition. An editorial "expert" often pounces ferociously on a trivial error of fact while passing calmly over the most arbitrary and irresponsible evaluative judgments. The explanation is that literary studies have felt keenly the impact of inductive science, but have remained insensitive to the development of value theory. The disciplines of fact-gathering are known; those of opinion-forming are not. The next step in the development of a sound critical methodology would therefore appear to be the growth of scrupulosity in an area of thought still dominated by individual caprice.

This caution having been uttered, we may move on to the observing of two variant methods of rendering total judgments. One is to make a single general demand on literature; the other is to require a cluster of distinct value properties. The appropriate instruments of measurement may be called, respectively, the yardstick and the score card.[3]

Much can be said in favor of the yardstick, since in

theory a single demand would appear to require less dialectic support than a multiple demand. If it should be decided, for example, that literature has no responsibility but that of achieving a tight organic unity, one will probably do better to stop there than to decide that the elements constituting the unity are limited in any special way. What counts is the quality, not the manner of the achievement. The isolation of a series of value properties which together are asserted to be constitutive of the quality opens the door to objections over and above those that can be brought against the demand for the quality. These considerations seemed to me decisive when I wrote the following:

> abstract definitions must be arrived at by a method which is not additive, but *penetrative*. The attempt is not to crowd more and more items into an increasingly wordy predication—not, that is to say, to lay a succession of partial definitions end to end—but to proceed from shallow formulations to deeper and deeper ones, until finally the deepest and most inclusive of all has been discovered.*

Yet it is questionable that reductionism should always go so far. The attempt to go beneath may insensibly transform itself into a compulsion to get rid of, with the result that simplicity is won at the expense of sincerity.

An illustration will clarify the point. "Good" beef cattle ought, by the consent of all interested persons, to provide tasty (and of course nutritious) meat in large amounts. How can this double demand be reduced to unity? A steer which yields large amounts of tough meat, or another which yields small amounts of tasty meat, is less than ideal. No ingenuity can reduce the ideas of quantity and quality to singleness, though in some languages—for example, Chinese—a word might be coined to mean "much-good."

What is true of beef cattle is true also of other objects to which human beings attach value—shoes, automobiles, pictures, radio-phonographs. A "good" shoe ought probably to be comfortable, made of durable materials, and of pleasing design. A "good" automobile might be agreed to be one with an efficient engine, attractive appearance, sturdy body construction, convenient appointments, and so on. Only the rare purchase of a car is decided by a single value property. Even if one property is especially desired (power or comfort), others will be taken for granted (the tires must hold air, the brakes grip, the headlights turn on). Neither, I think, can a series of demands usefully be reduced by substituting a single emotive term for a group of physically descriptive ones. Literature, which may sometimes be as complex as an automobile, must "satisfy": yes, but how is satisfaction to be construed? What, precisely, are the desires to be met, and what properties that analysis can establish to be present may be considered always capable of meeting the demands? Unless these questions can be answered, the domain of critical analysis threatens again to become that of intuitive, not rational, understanding. The critic may thus be forced back on the score card in spite of his vivid awareness of the greater convenience of the yardstick.

By such considerations one is led finally to a realization that judgments of total value inevitably include some estimate of quantity. Let us return to the example of the beef steer; instead of supposing that we make two separate demands on the steer (meat of superior quality and quantity), we can use the quantitative demand as a measure of the qualitative one. Whether the steer is valuable depends on whether it will yield good meat; the degree of its value is determinable by measurement of the quantity of value obtainable from it. Similarly, a shoe is durable only in comparison with other shoes. How long "ought" a good shoe to wear—a month, six months, five years? The question is answerable only in the light of experience with many shoes (that is, it leads to quantitative comparisons). In isolation it is as meaningless as an inquiry about an object we are unable to compare with known members of the same class. (How often ought a flying saucer to require servicing?) The qualities of comfort and pleasing design, although less accurately measurable, probably also contain a quantitative element. And so with the vast majority of value properties, if not with all. But, indeed (one gradually perceives), the assumption that every quality has an absolute form which can be established as present or absent is appropriate only to a Platonic or medieval realism. In modern thought there is almost everywhere a strong relativistic element.

The same line of reasoning applies to literary judgment. A literary style, for example, may be defined as good if it is adequate to express the author's subject, bad if it is inadequate to express the subject; but in fact expressiveness is not a quality without degrees. It resembles rather nutriment in the soil (there in some measure) than a light bulb in a socket (there or not there). Vividness and form, again, are not absolutes. There are degrees of vividness, degrees of organizational tightness. Only by assuming some zero point on a scale running up toward increasing goodness and down toward increasing badness can positive qualities be separated from negative ones.

This discovery is especially chilling. Few critics wish to measure degrees and percentages, to declare that a certain work scores eighty-three per cent and another only forty-seven per cent. In recent years the practice of granting every author his subject has led rather to the contrary emphasis, on uniqueness, idiosyncrasy, individuality. Nevertheless, it is certain that every judicial critic makes some use of quantitative standards. If he is unconscious of their existence, the reason is that they have established themselves insensibly, as a result of the interplay of his total literary experience and whatever convictions he holds about the nature of literary value. Thus again the haphazardness of the critical process forces itself upon our notice. The course of safety, obviously, would be either to describe one's evaluative scales carefully or deliberately to keep the range of one's evaluative epithets wide, so that the judgments will have the character rather of gestures to right or left than of exact indications of position.

For the rest, total evaluations depend on total definitions of value—definitions, that is, which specify the characteristics the value object must have in quantities higher than zero in order to be valuable. But the assumptive character of all such definitions has already been noticed. How, then, is one definition to be preferred to another?

Mere liking is no doubt practically important, but the aims of the present study require us to search for a rational criterion. One can be found, fortunately, in our earlier discovery that all reasoning is reasoning in a circle. Large circles, plainly, are preferable to small ones, for they leave fewer items of the total human experience unaccounted for and potentially troublesome. The items of experience excluded from a small circle must either be fitted into other circles which may come into conflict with the first at points of intersection or else must remain outside all the circles, hence not be objects of understanding at all. The ideal circle is therefore one which comprehends all experience, and the ideal total definition of literary value must be appropriate to a total world view. But rational world views, which our preliminary assumptions require us to prefer to intuitive ones, are philosophies. We are thus brought back to the view implied in the preceding chapter, that value definitions have stronger logical standing in proportion as the thought processes on which they rest come closer to synthesizing all the data of experience.

This conclusion is given strong support by the fact that the most authoritative critical documents of past ages have been those which were most harmonious with authoritative philosophies. Aristotle's *Poetics*—beyond question the most influential piece of literary criticism ever written—was so beautifully consonant with an accepted world view that it maintained its ground long after it had ceased to have relevance to the actual literary situation. Horace's *De Arte Poetica* also owed its prestige partly to its compatibility with the accepted philosophy of norms. When at length, in the late eighteenth century, the authority of formism began to yield to that of objective idealism, the bases of critical judgment shifted also. Critics like Jeffrey and Croker, who continued in the nineteenth century to evaluate by standards appropriate to an obsolescent philosophy, gradually lost standing, whereas the influence of Coleridge and other exponents of the new synthesis increased steadily. In the meantime a competitive philosophy, English empiricism, was preparing the way for a scholarship of meticulous historical research. And these examples are typical. I know of no really important piece of critical writing, either theoretical or practical, which was not consistent with contemporary philosophical thought.

It is not, of course, necessary that the critic himself work out the philosophy which is to suggest his evaluative assumptions. Even Aristotle inherited the greater part of his world view from his predecessors. Much will be gained, however, if the critic is both conscious of his assumptions and aware of their relation to a body of disciplined thought, for he will then be able to translate his perceptions more effectively into rational knowledge. In a paragraph which might have been written for me to insert here, Daiches says,

> The ideal criticism begins with a philosophic view of life as a whole, proceeds with the separating out of literary activity from human activity in general and the assessing of their mutual relations, deducing from this a norm of literary value, and concludes by the application of this standard to the individual instance. But few critics have the intellectual stamina to go through the whole process, though that need not prevent us from recognising this course as

the ideal one to be pursued and basing our own efforts on this recognition. We can attempt to enter the critical field at different stages in the process and, always keeping an undistorted perspective, make in this way some contribution to the whole. But any question we discuss, any judgment we pass or opinion we form, must have reference to the complete process; it is only by keeping our eye always on the relation of literature to the rest of activity that we can be prevented from lapsing into arid and unprofitable verbosity.[5]

These conclusions, arrived at by a train of reasoning quite different from our own, are so appropriate to the present context that they summarize almost everything that has been said in the last four chapters. The critic may indeed enter the field at any point; but if his evaluations are total they will inevitably imply what Daiches calls the complete process.

The inquiry has led us into a rarefied atmosphere. The advisability that total evaluations be the end product of reflections that embrace everything under the sun is not likely to give the critic a sense of buoyant assurance. If he feels depressed, as he well may, comfort is available in the realization that even after the reflections have been carried through they must end in an ideational construct which hangs on an immense "perhaps." It may be, after all, that the best practical course of action is to make all evaluations frankly conditional. "If musical sound is a quality of great poetry, then in one respect this poem . . ." "If it is agreed that unity within complexity is the condition of literary achievement . . ." "If literature must reflect accurately the best thought of its period about ultimate human problems . . ." When all is said, every appraisal is a statement of the relationship between a body of literary subject matter and an evaluative reference frame. If only the reference frame is sharply focused and its implications clearly understood, painstaking analysis of the literature will reveal the appropriate evaluation. Judgments rendered against any evaluative reference frame, no matter how trivial, will have something of the character of proved fact if only the reference frame is adequately acknowledged. Judgments rendered against concealed standards, however, will always appear arbitrary and, to those unconvinced by rhetoric or authority, meaningless.

Notes

CHAPTER 1.

[1] Joseph Shipley, *Dictionary of World Literature* (New York, Philosophical Library, Inc., 1943). Quotations used by permission of the publisher.

[2] The original French, German, and Italian passages follow: "dont il a pu quelquefois sembler qu'on aurait fait dans notre siècle le tout de la critique." Ferdinand Brunetiere, *La Grande Encyclopédie*, Vol. XIII, p. 417. "Die *literarisch-ästhetische* K. beschäftigt sich vorzugsweise mit der Prüfung, ob sich eine Schrift den zur Zeit ihrer Abfassung geltenden Gesetzen der Schönheit nach Form und Inhalt anpasst." *Der Grosse Brockhaus* (15th ed.), art. "Kritik." "Ogni atteggiamento e funzione dell'umano conoscere che miri a distinguere nel proprio oggetto ciò che in esso ha, comunque, valore da ciò che valore non ha." *Enciclopedia Italiana* (Instituto Giovanni Treccani, Milan, 1931–1939).

[3] "La critique littéraire consiste à analyser l'œuvre d'un écrivain, à l'expliquer par ses causes, à juger sa valeur esthétique." A. Ricardou, *La Critique littéraire: Etude philosophique* (Paris, 1896), p. 1.

[4] W. C. Brownell, *Criticism* (New York, Charles Scribner's Sons, 1914), pp. 16–17. Quotations used by permission of the publisher.

[5] J. M. Murry, *Aspects of Literature* (New York, Alfred A. Knopf, Inc., 1920). Quotations used by permission of the publisher.

[6] T. S. Eliot, *The Use of Poetry and the Use of Criticism* (London, Faber and Faber, 1933), p. 16. Quotations used by permission of the publisher.

[7] J. M. Robertson, *Essays towards a Critical Method* (London, 1889), p. 2.

[8] "Notre esthétique... aime mieux contempler que juger, étudier qu'apprécier; ou, si elle apprécie, c'est en laissant parler et se dérouler le sens intime d'une œuvre. Elle rend à chaque chose son lieu, à chaque lieu sa chose. Elle a renoncé au stérile procédé qui consiste à opposer une forme du beau à une autre, à préférer, à exclure. Elle n'a ni préjugé, ni parti pris. Elle croit tout, elle aime tout, elle supporte tout... Elle est vaste comme le monde, tolérante comme la nature." Schérer, quoted by Ricardou, *op. cit.*, p. 106, from *Revue des deux mondes*, February 15, 1861.

[9] Richard Moulton, *Shakespeare as a Dramatic Artist* (2d ed., Oxford, 1888), pp. 2–3.

[10] *Ibid.*, p. 4.

[11] *Ibid.*, pp. 17–18.

[12] Louis Cazamian, *Criticism in the Making* (New York, Macmillan Co., 1929), p. 26. Quotations used by permission of the publisher.

[13] R. P. Blackmur, "A Critic's Job of Work," *The Double Agent: Essays in Craft and Elucidation* (New York, Arrow Editions, 1935; to be reissued by Harcourt, Brace and Co.), pp. 269, 277. Quotations used by permission of the author.

[14] Stanley Edgar Hyman, *The Armed Vision: A Study in the Methods of Modern Literary Criticism* (New York, Alfred A. Knopf, Inc., 1948), p. 4. Quotations used by permission of the publisher.

[15] See *ibid.*, pp. 311–312, for a comment on this change of face.

CHAPTER 2.

[1] Louis Cazamian, *Criticism in the Making* (New York, Macmillan Co., 1929), pp. 28–29.

[2] *Ibid.*, p. 16.

[3] Stanley Edgar Hyman, *The Armed Vision* (New York, Knopf, 1948), p. 399.

[4] For the whole passage see *ibid.*, pp. 399–401.

[5] *Ibid.*, p. 401.

CHAPTER 3.

[1] It does not follow that thereafter the figure would be common knowledge among students of Hopkins' poetry or that everyone aware of the existence of the figure would refrain from making statements contrary to its implications. See George R. Stewart's article, "Truth Crushed to Earth at Gravelly Ford," *Pacific Spectator*, Vol. IV, No. 1 (Winter, 1950).

[2] D. W. Prall, *Aesthetic Analysis* (New York, Thomas Y. Crowell Co., 1936), p. 194. Quotations used by permission of the publisher.

[3] *Ibid.*, pp. 23–24.

[4] *Ibid.*, p. 34.

[5] See, for example, Part 2 of John Crowe Ransom's essay, "Poetry: The Final Cause," *Kenyon Review*, Vol. IX, No. 4 (Autumn, 1947).

[6] R. P. Blackmur, *The Double Agent* (New York, Arrow Editions, 1935), pp. 269–270.

[7] W. C. Brownell, *Criticism* (New York, Charles Scribner's Sons, 1914), pp. 70–71.

[8] The first phrase is the theme of an essay by John Crowe Ransom, "On Shakespeare's Language," *Sewanee Review*, Vol. LV, No. 2 (Spring, 1949), p. 181. The essay on Hardy's metaphors, by Allen Tate, is accessible in *Reason in Madness* (New York, G. P. Putnam's Sons, 1941).

[9] The essays referred to are the following, in order: Newell F. Ford, "Endymion—A Neo-Platonic Allegory?" *ELH*, Vol. XIV, No. 1 (March, 1947); Arthur O. Lovejoy, "Milton and the Paradox of the Fortunate Fall," *ibid.*, Vol. IV, No. 3 (September, 1937); Helmut Rehder, "Novalis and Shakespeare," *PMLA*, Vol. LXIII, No. 2, Part 1 (June, 1948); Wallace W. Douglas, "Wordsworth as Business Man," *ibid.*; Herbert E. Greene, "Browning's Knowledge of Music," *ibid.*, Vol. LXII, No. 4, Part 1 (December, 1947).

CHAPTER 4.

[1] Cited by J. M. Murry, *Aspects of Literature* (New York, Knopf, 1920), p. 2.

[2] London *Times*, Literary Supplement, May 27, 1949, p. 346.

[3] Louis Cazamian, *Criticism in the Making* (New York, Macmillan Co., 1929), p. 29.

[4] J. M. Robertson, *Essays towards a Critical Method* (London, 1889), p. 71.

[5] Mark Schorer, Josephine Miles, and Gordon McKenzie (eds.), *Criticism: The Foundations of Modern Literary Judgment* (New York, Harcourt, Brace and Co., 1948).

[6] Stanley Edgar Hyman, *The Armed Vision* (New York, Knopf, 1948), p. 398.

[7] Even Cazamian's classification, which opposes literary history to impressionism, leaves a large undistributed remainder. The division of criticisms into macroscopic, microscopic, and middle-distance is technically exhaustive, but in practice it would lead to the examination of "good" samples—one from each extreme and one from the exact middle, but none from the shadowy borderlines.

Chapter 5.

[1] D. W. Prall, *Aesthetic Analysis* (New York, Thomas Y. Crowell Co.), p. 23.

[2] Richard Moulton, *The Modern Study of Literature: An Introduction to Literary Theory and Interpretation* (Chicago, 1915), chap. v.

[3] *Ibid.*, p. 99.

[4] René Wellek and Austin Warren, *Theory of Literature* (New York, Harcourt, Brace and Co., 1949), p. 65. Quotations used by permission of the publisher.

[5] *Ibid.*, p. 139.

[6] For example, Douglas Bush refers to himself as a "simple-minded seeker of light," an "untouchable," and a "mere scholar." See "The New Criticism: Some Old-fashioned Queries," *PMLA*, Vol. LXIV, Suppl., Part 2 (March, 1949), pp. 13–21. The quoted phrases are from p. 14.

[7] F. R. Leavis, "The Literary Discipline and Liberal Education," *Sewanee Review*, Vol. LV, No. 3 (Autumn, 1947), p. 586.

[8] Louis Cazamian, *Criticism in the Making* (New York, Macmillan Co., 1929), pp. vii–viii.

[9] Cf. R. P. Blackmur's observation: "No critic is required to limit himself to a single approach, nor is he likely to be able to do so; facts cannot be exhibited without comment, and comment involves the generality of the mind." "A Critic's Job of Work," *The Double Agent* (New York, Arrow Editions, 1935), p. 278.

[10] Classifications by other writers seem to be oriented in special directions, so as not to fit the present context, or to be offhand and perfunctory, capable of supporting the structure of a paragraph or two but not that of a chapter or book.

[11] Quoted by Fraser Neiman in "Milton's *Sonnet XX*," *PMLA*, Vol. LXIV, No. 3, Part 1 (June, 1949), p. 481.

[12] Edwin Greenlaw, *The Province of Literary History* (Baltimore, Johns Hopkins University Press, 1931), p. 128.

[13] Louis Harap, *Social Roots of the Arts* (New York, International Publishers Co., Inc., 1949), p. 55. Quotations used by permission of the publisher.

[14] John Ruskin, *Modern Painters*, Vol. II.

[15] Quoted by Stanley Edgar Hyman, *The Armed Vision* (New York, Knopf, 1948), p. 265.

CHAPTER 6.

[1] J. E. Spingarn, *The New Criticism: A Lecture Delivered at Columbia University March 9, 1910* (New York, 1911), p. 31.

[2] Cleanth Brooks, "Criticism and Literary History: Marvell's Horatian Ode," *Sewanee Review*, Vol. LV, No. 2 (Spring, 1947), p. 222.

[3] D. W. Prall, *Aesthetic Analysis* (New York, Thomas Y. Crowell Co., 1936), p. 25.

[4] "Du temps de La Harpe on était grammairien, du temps de Sainte-Beuve et de Taine on est historien. Quand sera-t-on artiste, rien qu'artiste, mais bien artiste? Où connaissez-vous une critique qui s'inquiète de l'œuvre en *soi* d'une façon intense?" Quoted by A. Ricardou, *La Critique littéraire* (Paris, 1896), p. 25.

[5] "L'histoire littéraire dont l'instrument est la méthode historique a évidemment une grande importance. Elle peut nous montrer dans son évolution l'esprit d'un peuple et même de l'humanité, mais elle atteint cette fin en obscurcissant la fin propre de la littérature." Michel Dragomirescou, *La Science de la littérature* (Paris, 1928–1929), Vol. I, p. 8.

[6] "... allusions à des faits contemporains, tout ce réseau si dense qui peut unir l'œuvre à ce qui n'est pas elle, tout ce bagage historique dont sont surchargées les notes de nos éditions scolaires et surtout savantes." The sentence is Van Tieghem's—see p. 45 of the work next to be cited—but is accurately descriptive of Dragomirescou's scorn of historical scholarship.

[7] Philippe Van Tieghem, *Tendances nouvelles en histoire littéraire* (Paris, Société d'Edition "Les Belles Lettres," 1930). Quotations used by permission of the publisher.

[8] "... ne sont pas des signes d'autre chose qu'elles; elles sont des signes de soi, qui n'expriment en théorie rien qu'elles-mêmes." *Ibid.* (P. 51.) "Il y a des gens qui vont au spectacle pour observer le public, et, toujours, le public du poulailler, avec ses réactions vives." (P. 53.) "... l'important est, à mon avis, de se placer avant tout dans le texte, d'y rester aux aguets, de prendre chaque mot, chaque effet, chaque phrase pour en retrouver la valeur; il faut trouver les rapports et dégager l'harmonie fondée sur eux, faire voir mille nuances de sentiment ou de pénsee où le vulgaire n'aperçoit qu'une heureuse expression, dégager une beauté de détail que l'auteur a négligé de mettre en valeur; montrer la portée des idées qu'il aurait pu approfondir ou développer sans détruire les proportions ou choquer les lois du genre, analyser les multiples éléments d'un état d'âme dont l'auteur ne nous a livré que la vivante synthèse." (P. 56.)

[9] To what degree this is true can perhaps most easily be seen by reading the chapters on the intrinsic approaches to literature in *Theory of Literature* (New York, Harcourt, Brace and Co., 1949), by René Wellek and Austin Warren.

[10] "Il est vain de dire que vous ne formez aucune hypothèse, car vous ne sauriez vous engager dans une recherche sans être guidé par un certain plan, un certain parti pris, une certaine attente, ou la décision de vous en tenir à une certaine époque, ce qui déjà est un jugement et une hypothèse. ... L'une des plus grandes faiblesses de l'histoire littéraire scientifique me semble être d'ignorer l'usage de l'hypothèse et de cher-

cher à s'en passer." Van Tieghem, *op. cit.*, p. 14. The passage should be read in its context in a lively and penetrating article: Bernard Faÿ, "Doutes et réflexions sur l'étude de la littérature," *Romanic Review*, Vol. XIX, No. 2 (April–June, 1928). See also Leslie Fiedler: "The 'pure' literary critic, who pretends, in the cant phrase, to stay 'inside' a work all of whose metaphors and meanings are pressing outward, is only half-aware. And half-aware, he deceives; for he cannot help smuggling unexamined moral and metaphysical judgments into his 'close analyses,' any more than the 'pure' literary historian can help bootlegging unconfessed aesthetic estimates into his chronicles. Literary criticism is always becoming 'something else,' for the simple reason that literature is always 'something else.'" "My Credo: A Symposium of Critics," *Kenyon Review*, Vol. XII, No. 4 (Autumn, 1950), p. 564. Quotations used by permission of John Crowe Ransom, editor of the *Kenyon Review*.

[11] Professor Kittredge's study was published by the Chaucer Society in 1891; Miss Rickert's in Chicago in 1927. Some readers may be surprised that I admit linguistic studies and statistical tables to the discussion. Why not, if they fall, as these do, within the terms of our governing definition of criticism?

[12] Cleanth Brooks, "The Language of Paradox," *The Language of Poetry* (a symposium), ed. Allen Tate (Princeton, N. J., Princeton University Press, 1942), p. 38.

[13] Thus Robert Wooster Stallman, in the preface to an anthology of recent critical essays, says that the "new" critics, "by confining their strategy to the literary work itself," have at once restricted the scope of criticism and illuminated its center. *Critiques and Essays in Criticism, 1920–1948* (New York, Ronald Press Co., 1949), p. v. But contrast with this view the decision of William Barrett, agreed to by Allen Tate, that "there have been New Critics, but no such thing as *the* New Criticism." *The American Scholar*, Vol. XX, No. 1 (Winter, 1950–1951), p. 98.

[14] "Les œuvres littéraires se rouillent et deviennent ternes après un certain temps d'usage. Il faut les vivifier. Pour ça, les reprendre d'un point de vue original. ... Il faut les illuminer sans cesse d'hypothèses variées qui les éclairent vivement et leur prêtent une vie jeune à mesure que leur sève s'épuise." Quoted by Van Tieghem, *op. cit.*, p. 17.

[15] Richard Moulton, *The Modern Study of Literature* (Chicago, 1915), p. 295.

[16] J. E. Spingarn, *Creative Criticism and Other Essays* (new enl. ed., New York, Harcourt, Brace and Co., 1931), p. 167. Quotations used by permission of the publisher.

[17] Louis Cazamian, *Criticism in the Making* (New York, Macmillan Co., 1929), pp. 32–33.

[18] Prall, *op. cit.*, p. 2.

[19] W. K. Wimsatt, Jr., and M. C. Beardsley, "The Intentional Fallacy," *Sewanee Review*, Vol. LIV, No. 3 (Summer, 1946), pp. 468–488.

[20] Prall, *op. cit.*, p. 165.

[21] "Il se produit ce fait étonnant qu'il est plus agréable et plus vraiment instructif de parler de Stendhal ou de Dante avec tel homme cultivé, plein de goût et de réflexion ... qu'avec tel spécialiste qui a fait tant de recherches sur Stendhal, ou tel autre qui est si étonnant sur la politique des Blancs et des Noirs." Van Tieghem, *op. cit.*, p. 59.

[22] Robert Wooster Stallman, "Hardy's Hour-Glass Novel," *Sewanee Review*, Vol. LV, No. 2 (Spring, 1947), pp. 283–296.

[23] E. M. Forster, *Aspects of the Novel* (New York, 1927).

[24] William Empson, *Some Versions of Pastoral* (London, Chatto and Windus, 1935), pp. 119–145.

[25] R. P. Warren, "Pure and Impure Poetry," *Kenyon Review*, Vol. V, No. 2 (Spring, 1943), pp. 228–254.

CHAPTER 7.

[1] Kenneth Burke, *Counter-Statement* (New York, 1931), p. 235.

[2] Louis Cazamian, *Criticism in the Making* (New York, Macmillan Co., 1929), p. vii.

[3] "... devient absolument nuisible lorsqu'il s'agit de l'étude des chefs-d'œuvre." Michel Dragomirescou, *La Science de la littérature* (Paris, 1928–1929), Vol. I, p. 31.

[4] W. C. Brownell, *Criticism* (New York, Charles Scribner's Sons, 1914), p. 57.

[5] "Observe, I neither impugn nor doubt the conclusions of the science, if its terms are accepted. I am simply uninterested in them, as I should be in those of a science of gymnastics which assumed that men had no skeletons." John Ruskin, *The Political Economy of Art, Unto This Last, Sesame and Lilies, The Crown of Wild Olive* (London, 1912), p. 124.

[6] Herbert Read, *The Grassroots of Art* (New York, Wittenborn and Co., 1947).

CHAPTER 8.

[1] *The American College Dictionary* (New York and London, Harper and Bros., 1947).

[2] Rudolf Arnheim, "The Priority of Expression," *Journal of Aesthetics and Art Criticism*, Vol. VIII, No. 2 (December, 1949), p. 106.

[3] I. A. Richards, *Practical Criticism: A Study of Literary Judgment* (London, Routledge and Kegan Paul, Ltd., sixth impression, 1948), p. 11.

[4] I owe this suggestion to Bertram Jessup, Professor of Philosophy at the University of Oregon.

[5] "Seit den griechischen und römischen Ethikern des Altertums hat es wohl keine Zeit gegeben, in welcher die Werttheorie, und was an Problemen sachlich mit ihr zusammenhängt, so sehr im Blickfelde der allgemeinen Aufmerksamkeit gestanden wäre, wie gegenwärtig." Christian von Ehrenfels, *System der Werttheorie* (Leipzig, 1897), p. v.

[6] J. F. Dashiell, *The Philosophical Status of Values* (New York, 1913), p. 11.

[7] C. E. Ayres, "The Value Economy," in *Value: A Coöperative Inquiry*, ed. Ray Lepley (New York, Columbia University Press, 1949), p. 49.

[8] The volume cited in the preceding footnote.

[9] Abraham Kaplan, "On the So-called Crisis in Criticism," *Journal of Aesthetics and Art Criticism*, Vol. VII, No. 1 (September, 1948), pp. 42–48. Quotations used by permission of Thomas Munro, editor of the *Journal of Aesthetics and Art Criticism*.

[10] *Ibid.*, p. 42.

[11] *Ibid.*

[12] *Ibid.*

[13] J. M. Murry, *Aspects of Literature* (New York, Knopf, 1920), p. 8.

[14] Kaplan, *op. cit.*, pp. 42–43.

[15] Ralph Barton Perry, *General Theory of Value: Its Meaning and Basic Principles Construed in Terms of Interest* (New York and London, 1926), p. 18. Quotations used by permission of Harvard University Press, present holder of the copyright.

[16] Kaplan, *op. cit.*, p. 43.

[17] *Ibid.*, pp. 43–44.

[18] Cf. D. W. Prall, *Aesthetic Analysis* (New York, Thomas Y. Crowell Co., 1936), p. 173: "Aesthetic analysis, as its groundwork has been sketched in these chapters, offers explicitly no critically determining principles." See also Bertram E. Jessup, "On Value," in *Value: A Coöperative Inquiry*, p. 133: "A description of an object (though it may do so on the basis of implicit value assumptions) never strictly denotes value."

[19] Jessup, *op. cit.*, p. 139.

[20] Cf. Stephen C. Pepper, *A Digest of Purposive Values* (Berkeley and Los Angeles, University of California Press, 1947), p. 77: "The criterion for determining the qualitative judgment for any kind of value is the definition of that kind of value. . . . This definition is the ultimate criterion of value for the type of value defined." See also George Boas, *A Primer for Critics* (Baltimore, Johns Hopkins University Press, 1937), p. 149: "Every work of art is multivalent and the 'real' aesthetic value is a matter of definition only."

CHAPTER 9.

[1] *The American College Dictionary* (New York and London, Harper and Bros., 1947).

[2] Stephen C. Pepper, *The Basis of Criticism in the Arts* (Cambridge, Mass., Harvard University Press, 1945), p. 25.

[3] *Ibid.*

[4] Ralph Barton Perry, *General Theory of Value* (New York and London, 1926), p. 22.

[5] Pepper, *op. cit.*, pp. 30–31.

[6] The dependence of each of the philosophies on a root metaphor is discussed at length by Stephen C. Pepper in *World-Hypotheses* (Berkeley and Los Angeles, University of California Press, 1942), chap. v.

[7] Bertram E. Jessup, "On Value," in *Value: A Coöperative Inquiry*, ed. Ray Lepley (New York, Columbia University Press, 1949), p. 128.

[8] Lewis Hahn, "A Contextualist Looks at Values," in *ibid.*, p. 112.

[9] Perry, *op. cit.*, p. 75.

[10] T. S. Eliot, "Hamlet and His Problems," *Selected Essays, 1917–1932* (New York, Harcourt, Brace and Co., 1932), p. 123.

[11] Thus Henry Osborn Taylor, in *Human Values and Verities* (London, Macmillan and Co., Ltd., 1928), p. 117, note, quotes G. N. Lewis as querying whether there is "any such thing as absolutely rigorous proof. Is not a proof only an attempt to render plausible new statements by correlating them with others that are already accepted?" (*Anatomy of Science*, pp. 90, 94).

[12] Mark Schorer *et al.* (eds.), *Criticism: The Foundations of Modern Literary Judgment* (New York, Harcourt, Brace and Co., 1948), p. vii.

[13] The two things come together in the end, for Trollope identified the morally pleasing with the lifelike. Miss Broughton's characters, he wrote in a remarkable sentence, "are not sweet-savoured as are those by Miss Thackeray, and are, therefore, less true to nature." Anthony Trollope, *Autobiography*, World's Classics ed. (London, 1936), p. 235.

[14] J. F. Dashiell, *The Philosophical Status of Values* (New York, 1913), p. 68.

[15] H. Osborne, *Foundations of the Philosophy of Value: An Examination of Value and Value Theories* (Cambridge University Press, 1933), p. 12.

CHAPTER 10.

[1] David Daiches, *New Literary Values: Studies in Modern Literature* (Edinburgh and London, Oliver and Boyd, 1936), p. 116. Quotations used by permission of the publisher.

[2] David Daiches, *A Study of Literature for Readers and Critics* (Ithaca, N. Y., Cornell University Press, 1948), p. 58.

[3] This is the secondary classification mentioned in the text.

[4] Percy Lubbock, *The Craft of Fiction* (New York, Jonathan Cape, Ltd., and Harrison Smith, 1931), pp. 23–24. Quotations used by permission of the publisher.

[5] It is evident that this discussion has been fragmentary and superficial. Persons who wish to supplement it are advised to go first to Stephen C. Pepper, *The Basis of Criticism in the Arts* (Cambridge, Mass., Harvard University Press, 1945), which I have already cited as the source for the structure, and in part the content, of my summary, and then to the volumes mentioned by Pepper as classic treatments of the four types of aesthetic theory: Bernard Bosanquet's *Three Lectures on Aesthetic*, Aristotle's *Poetics*, George Santayana's *The Sense of Beauty*, and John Dewey's *Art as Experience*. To these may be added Pepper's *Aesthetic Quality* (New York, Charles Scribner's Sons, 1938), which deserves to stand beside the others as an excellent statement of one of the four points of view (the contextualist).

[6] The positive argument is by W. K. Wimsatt, the negative by Theodore M. Green. *Journal of Aesthetics and Art Criticism*, Vol. VIII, No. 4 (June, 1950), pp. 213–220, 221–228.

[7] Samuel Alexander, *Beauty and Other Forms of Value* (London, Macmillan and Co., Ltd., 1933), pp. 148, 137–138.

[8] "Une œuvre littéraire est d'autant plus belle qu'elle exprime plus de vérité et de moralité en une forme plus puissante." A. Ricardou, *La Critique littéraire* (Paris, 1896), p. 270.

[9] Henry Osborn Taylor, *Human Values and Verities* (London, Macmillan and Co., Ltd., 1928), pp. 208–209.

[10] Daiches, *New Literary Values*, p. 8.

[11] J. M. Murry, *Aspects of Literature* (New York, Knopf, 1920), p. 176.

CHAPTER 11.

[1] R. W. Short, "Some Critical Terms of Henry James," *PMLA*, Vol. LXV, No. 5 (September, 1950), pp. 667–668.

[2] T. S. Eliot's essay, "Milton," reprinted from *Proceedings of the British Academy*, Vol. XXXIII, in James Thorpe, *Milton Criticism: Selections from Four Centuries* (New York, Rinehart and Co., Inc., 1950), pp. 316–317.

[3] I borrow the terms from E. T. Mitchell, "Values, Valuing, and Evaluation," in *Value: A Coöperative Inquiry*, ed. Ray Lepley (New York, Columbia University Press, 1949), p. 198. His two additional terms, the "ideal" and the "hypothesis," I do not use because the latter seems to be irrelevant to literary judgment and the former to be implicit in the use of yardsticks or score cards.

[4] Wayne Shumaker, "The Condition of Critical Valuation," *Journal of Aesthetics and Art Criticism*, Vol. IX, No. 1 (September, 1950), p. 26.

[5] David Daiches, *New Literary Values* (Edinburgh and London, Oliver and Boyd, 1936), p. 10.

CPSIA information can be obtained
at www.ICGtesting.com
Printed in the USA
LVHW042235120922
728185LV00006B/315